GEMS OF TRUTH & BEAUTY

SPURGEON | MOODY | BEECHER
GUTHRIE | PARKER | TALMAGE

www.gideonhousebooks.com

Gems of Truth and Beauty

Charles Spurgeon, D.L. Moody, Charles C. Albertson

© 2016 Gideon House Books

All rights reserved. No part of this publication may be reproduced, stored in a retrieval system or transmitted in any form or by any means, electronic, mechanical, photocopying, recording or otherwise without the prior permission of the publisher or in accordance with the provisions of the Copyright, Designs and Patents Act 1988 or under the terms of any licence permitting limited copying issued by the Copyright Licensing Agency.

Published by:
Gideon House Books
2137 Ash Grove Way
Dallas, TX 75228

ISBN-13: 978-1-943133-43-7

Also from Gideon House Books

The Sovereignty of God by A.W. Pink
A Christian on the Mount by Andrew Murray
The Mission of Sorrow by Gardiner Spring
Missionary Methods: St. Paul's or Ours? by Roland Allen
Humility: The Beauty of Holiness by Andrew Murray
The Essentials of Prayer by E.M. Bounds
Till He Come by C.H. Spurgeon
Sovereign Grace by D.L. Moody
God's Light in Dark Clouds by Theodore Cuyler
A Church in the House by Matthew Henry
Indwelling Sin in Believers by John Owen
Secret Power by D.L. Moody
Thoughts for Young Men by J.C. Ryle
The Divine Liturgy of St. John Chrysostom
A Study on Dispensationalism by A.W. Pink
Prevailing Prayer: What Hinders It by D.L. Moody
The Duty of Pastors by John Owen
The Expulsive Power of a New Affection by Thomas Chalmers
According to Promise by Charles Spurgeon
The Resurrection: A Symposium by Charles Spurgeon
The Acceptable Sacrifice by John Bunyan

Find these titles and more at
www.gideonhousebooks.com

Contents

Introduction 9	Death 101
Biographical Sketches 11	Decision 105
Access To God 23	Divinity Of Christ 109
Activity 27	Duty 113
Adoption 31	Earnestness 117
Affliction 35	Education 121
Atonement 39	Eternity 125
The Bible 43	Faith 127
The Blood Of Jesus 47	Forgiveness 131
Brotherly Love 51	Friendship 135
Charity 55	God 137
Cheerfulness 59	The Gospel 141
Children 63	Grace 145
Christ 67	Heaven 147
Confession 71	Holiness 151
Conscience 75	Holy Spirit 155
Consolation 79	Home 159
Conversion 83	Hope 161
Courage 87	Humility 163
Creation 91	Infidelity 165
The Cross 93	Intemperance 169
Cross-bearing 97	Judgment 173

Life.. 177	Reward...................................... 247
Little Things............................ 181	Riches 251
Love 185	Sabbath 255
Man 189	Self-denial 257
Marriage.................................... 193	Sin.. 259
Missions.................................... 197	The Church.............................. 263
Mother...................................... 201	The Soul Immortal 267
Old Age..................................... 205	Tongue....................................... 271
Patience..................................... 209	Woman 275
Poor 213	Youth 279
Power 217	
Prayer 221	
Preaching 225	
Procrastination 231	
Punishment............................... 235	
Resurrection 239	
Rest.. 243	

Introduction

The age in which we live demands both variety and brevity in much that we read. People wish to compass many subjects in the shortest time. This disposition arises largely, no doubt, from the necessities and opportunities of our civilization. The improved appliances of business, the increased facilities for travel, and the wonderful rapidity with which we gather information, render it indispensable that there be periodicals, and at least some books which present the freshest and best thoughts in convenient and concise form.

The pages of "GEMS OF TRUTH AND BEAUTY," show it to be a book of this kind. The author has skillfully selected from some of the greatest preachers, among the dead and living, many of their choicest sayings. Some of these sayings are the result of the most careful elaboration in the study, others are the sudden flashes of inspiration in moments of high excitement; but whether coming to their originators suddenly or slowly, they have back of them the power of experience and culture. Thus, the reader of this volume, if seated in the quiet of his house, or rushing over the country at lightning speed, can commune with the best thoughts of Guthrie, Beecher, Spurgeon, Parker, Talmage and Moody, and feel something of the glow which these men have imparted to the audiences which have sat or still sit in rapt attention upon their ministrations.

A single sentence which the mind takes in with even a casual reading may be enough to start a whole train of devout and helpful reflections, as when an unexpected gap in a chain of mountains opens a long vista of plain and valley, or a sudden rift in the clouds discloses a well-nigh infinite expanse of sky.

It has been suggested that the way to make reading more agreeable is to make it rather desultory. Especially if the mind is largely occupied with the perplexing affairs of business, and needs recreation, or if one wishes to pass the time pleasantly on a railway train, it is desirable to peruse a variety of reading. Both these advantages are met in "GEMS OF TRUTH AND

BEAUTY." In it the mind may course over a large variety of topics all of which are presented with the interest which a quick succession of themes and a great diversity of authorship affords. Then, too, so pure and elevated are the topics treated—Christ, His salvation, the love of God, humanity, liberty, and related subjects, and so forcible and beautiful the style in which they are clothed, that one cannot rise from this perusal without a corresponding elevation of thought and feeling.

In no better society can one spend his hours than in communion with such a book, a friend indeed, with whom one may converse not only without effort or weariness, but with ever recurring satisfaction and profit.

Henry B. Ridgaway.
Evanston, Ill., Jan. 2, 1890

BIOGRAPHICAL SKETCHES

T. DE WITT TALMAGE, D.D.

The subject of this sketch was born in New Jersey in 1882. He was the youngest of a family of twelve children. His parents were persons of pure Christian character, the fruits of whose judicious training were manifest in the conversion of DeWitt when eighteen years of age. He received his literary training in the University of New York, and afterward graduated from the theological school at New Brunswick, N. J. The first three years of his ministerial career were spent in Belleville, N. J., from whence he was called to Syracuse, N. T. After laboring here three years, he went to Philadelphia, where he remained seven years, during which time he earned a high place among the preachers of that city. His congregations were large, and his church rapidly increased in membership until it became widely known as the popular church of the city. Many large and important congregations were now extending calls to him. He accepted a call from the Central Presbyterian Church of Brooklyn, then in a state of decline, in preference to others, because he saw in Brooklyn an opportunity to build up a free church.

At the end of a year and a half the old edifice could no longer accommodate the congregations, and a tabernacle was built, and dedicated in September, 1870. This building which originally was designed to seat 3,000 persons, was enlarged a few months later. Just before the hour of service, December 22, 1872, the tabernacle was burned. In a few minutes, several churches were offered to the congregation for occupancy until their own house could be restored. The Academy of Music was engaged until a still larger structure, which still stands, was built to take the place of the old. This building has been recently enlarged until it now accommodates nearly 6,000 persons. The tabernacle is crowded at every service. Besides the regular congregation, Dr.

Talmage preaches to several millions through the press of the United States, Europe and Australia, which publishes his sermons regularly.

The published works of Dr. T aim age, which are numerous, have met with an immense sale. He is also in great demand as a lecturer, but makes all other things subordinate to his ministerial work. Personally, he is one of the most modest and unassuming of men. His appearance is not all clerical, but more resembles a prosperous business man. He is of pleasant address and sociable disposition. He is not only a preacher among preachers, but a man among men.

HENRY WARD BEECHER

Henry Ward Beecher was born in Litchfield, Connecticut, June 24, 1813. He was the son of the illustrious Dr. Lyman Beecher, and one of a family of thirteen children, several of whom have become world-renowned on account of abilities, literary and oratorical. His sister, Harriet Beecher Stowe, author of "Uncle Tom's Cabin," and his brother Edward, the author of "Conflict of Ages" are immortal on the roll of "mighty wielders of the pen for God and man."

In 1834 young Beecher graduated from Amherst with a poor grade, and pursued theological studies in Lane Seminary, at Cincinnati, then in charge of his father. In 1887 he accepted a call to become pastor of a church in Lawrenceburg, Indiana, and from there he was soon called to Indianapolis, whence, after serving nearly eight years, he went to Plymouth Church, Brooklyn, where his fame became world-wide as a bold and fearless advocate of truth in every line, in the pulpit, through the press, or on the platform.

In the campaign of 1856, Hr. Beecher openly advocated the Republican party, and addressed many public political gatherings. In the long, and trying period of the war, he championed the Union cause at home and abroad. Probably his most wonderful oratorical achievements were in England, when in 1863, he visited that country on a vacation, but was urged to address meetings in London, Manchester, Glasgow, Edinburgh, and Liverpool, defending the Union cause in an exposition of the principles which underlay the civil war.

As a preacher, Dr. Beecher was a prince. As one who sat under his ministry said: "Every word tells. His logic is dear. The unexpected descent which he makes upon errors of thought and conduct, frequently excites laughter, yet gravity sits upon him with a native grace. But his imagination is so rich and strong, his flow of language is so great, and the heart that beats like a great hammer in his breast, is such a volcanic hearty so impetuous, so prone to overflow, that he does sometimes lose the reins of prudence. The temperament which God gave a man must be considered in judging him; and, considering that of Mr. Beecher, also the multitude of things that he has said, and is forever saying, it is a proof that he possesses a remarkable share of discretion that he has said *so few* imprudent things as he has said."

Mr. Beecher was the most out-and-out American preacher our times have produced. His congregation, the Plymouth Church, was not only a sincerely religious organization, but a deeply patriotic one as well. It will go down in history as such. In the pulpit of that church national battles were fought, and national victories won.

The preacher's life and character have become so well-known, and, since his death, March 18, 1887, so many rich eulogies have been pronounced upon him that his is a name which needs no encomium. The world knows him. The world reveres his name.

CHARLES H. SPURGEON

Charles H. Spurgeon was born at Kelvedon, in Essex, June 19,1884. He came of a clerical ancestry, his father and grandfather both being ministers. He received his early education at Colchester, and also spent a year in the Agricultural College at Maidstone, where he obtained some knowledge of the sciences. He then engaged as usher in a school at Newmarket, after which he moved to Cambridge and served in a similar capacity in a day school, all the while employing his leisure in improving his own mind. He began, while at Newmarket, to make Sunday-school addresses, and it is said that he did it in a manner to attract older persons. At Cambridge he continued the custom, and also began to give Sunday-school sermons in surrounding villages. A small Baptist church at Waterbeach extended the young preacher a call, to be its pastor. He accepted the invitation, and during a short ministry the church was doubled. In January, 1854, when Mr. Spurgeon was but twenty years old, he was invited to accept the pastorate of New Park Street Chapel in London. He immediately began a career of Christian endeavor in that city which surpasses the record of almost any modem apostle we could name. Coming to the busy city fresh from quiet fields of study, observation and thought, with a vigor and power of expression, startling in their novelty, he at once arrested the attention of the people. Throngs came out to hear him. The church must be enlarged, and in order to accommodate the eager multitudes, he preached many sermons In the open air to fifteen thousand persons, and often in Exeter Hall to more than that number. Beginning his public career thus early in life, public interest in him has not for a moment waned. He is a preacher of the Gospel In its simplicity, and an orator of wonderful power. His pulpit work is supplemented by vast philanthropic and charitable enterprises, asylums, orphanages and schools. His published works are many, among which are "John Ploughman's Talks," "John Ploughman's Pictures," "Commenting and Commentaries," "Gleanings among the Sheaves," beside ten volumes of sermons. Perhaps the best known and most highly valued literary work of Mr. Spurgeon is his "Treasury of David," an exhaustive and helpful treatise on the Psalms.

Mr. Spurgeon's career has been phenomenal from his youthful entrance into the ministry until to-day. The work he has done for the Master in bringing souls to know Christ, and in strengthening believers in the faith will never be fully known until eternity.

DWIGHT L. MOODY

Dwight L. Moody, whose name shall be immortal in history as the Evangelist of the Nineteenth Century, was born at Northfield, Mass., February 5, 1837. His early home was a large frame-house a little distance from the town. His father, by farming a few acres, and working at his trade, which was that of a stone-mason was enabled to earn a comfortable living for his family, in which there were seven children, of whom Dwight was the youngest. Financial losses from an unfortunate business enterprise, were followed by the sudden death of the father, when Dwight was but four years old. A month later a twin boy and girl were born. But Mrs. Moody bore with a brave heart the weight of the family cares which were enough to crush an ordinary woman, and steadfastly refused to part from any of her children.

From this early training of poverty and self-denial, Dwight grew up a sturdy, healthy, self-reliant boy. He was so full of animal spirits, and liked fun so much more than study, that his record in school was poor. Yet he was in no sense stupid. He was observant, watchful, and susceptible to lessons learned from real life or nature.

At the age of seventeen, he set off from Northfield with a little money, to Seek his fortune in Boston. After considerable search for employment, his uncle, Samuel S. Holton, a shoe merchant agreed to hire him at a small salary. He soon became an attendant at the Congregational Church. Through the direct personal effort of his teacher in the Sunday-school he was converted, and gave himself to the service of God. At the age of twenty, Mr. Moody left Boston for Chicago, in order that he might have a more extended field of opportunity for working in the Master's cause. He found it. As teacher in Sunday-school, as street-solicitor for scholars, as mission-worker among sailors, visitor to prisons and hospitals, his work was constant and self-denying. A little later he hired a vacant room in a degraded portion of the city, and, gathering around him crowds of abandoned men and women, and unfortunate children, he preached the gospel to them and saved many souls. A large room became necessary, and within a year the average attendance at his Sunday-school was 650.

About the year 1860, Hr. Moody resolved to give himself up to the labor of saving souls, and to devote his entire time to the work of an Evangelist. A little later, he was made city missionary of the Young Men's Christian Association, and immediately began to make longer tours over the city assisting destitute families, and praying with many.

In 1861, the outbreak of the civil war extended the sphere of his activities. He became active in the organisation of a system of visitation and prayer-meetings among the troops gathered in Camp Douglas, near the city of Chicago. After the fall of Donelson, in February, 1862, he was sent to bear the consolations of religion to wounded and dying volunteers. Many of his most vivid and impressive illustrations are drawn from incidents in his experience on the battle-field.

In 1862 he was married to Miss Emma C. Revell. His wife was an active worker in missions and hence in thorough harmony with his self-denying life. To them have been born two children, Emma and Willie.

In 1868 a large house of worship was erected for his Sunday-school and congregation. This edifice was burned in the great fire of 1871. Mr. Moody then went East, holding revival services in Brooklyn, Philadelphia, and elsewhere, receiving contributions to rebuild his church. He was thus enabled to build a wooden Tabernacle on the old site, of mammoth size. One thousand children were present on the Sunday after it was finished. Finding the demand for Evangelistic labor in other fields urgent, he began to visit other cities and churches and hold special religious services. In nearly all the large cities of the Union, he has labored successfully. In 1871, he met Mr. Ira D. Sankey the sweet singer, and soon united him to himself as a co-worker in the ripened harvest field. Together they labored in America, England, Ireland, Scotland and both at home and abroad created such a revival of religious interest as this century has not seen before.

A devout student of the word, uneducated except in the art of saving souls, intensely earnest, untiring in activity, Dwight L. Moody has done much to bring the world to know Him. "whom to know is life eternal."

THOMAS GUTHRIE, D. D.

Thomas Guthrie was born at Brechin, in Forfarshire, July 12,1803. His father was a merchant and a banker, and the family was one of great respectability and antiquity. Thomas Guthrie was a lineal descendant of the well-known Dr. William Guthrie, author of "Trial of a Saying Interest in Christ," and who was a cousin of James Guthrie the martyr. Thomas was one of a family of several boys. Alexander, an elder brother, was a medical practitioner of considerable reputation. Charles, another brother, was a soldier in the Indian army, became a captain, and was killed in the first Burmese war. Until he was eleven years of age Thomas pursued his studies in his native town, but at that early period, as was the custom of the time, he was sent to the University of Edinburg. Having decided to enter the University, he passed through the Divinity Hall, and while yet very young, he was licensed as a preacher by the Presbytery of Brechin. It is by no means certain through whose influence he was led to choose the ministry as his profession, but it is very probable that his mother, who was, like Susannah Wesley," both a godly and a clever woman," disposed his youthful mind to it.

Though a licensed preacher, he was only a probationer, and for several years, for various reasons, he did not become pastor of a settled congregation. During this period he engaged in secular pursuits, assisted his father in the bank, and afterward paid some attention to the study of medicine.

In 1830, the parish of Arbirlot became vacant, and after considerable delay, Dr. Guthrie was settled as the minister. His talent as a preacher now began to appear. He set out with a firm purpose to make himself understood, and to gain and keep the attention of the people. This he did by giving especial attention to the illustrations in every sermon. His ministrations roused the people of that city into a vividness of religious thought and a seal for spiritual advancement. But the fame of the preacher had spread, and in 1837, Dr. Guthrie was elected to fill the vacancy in the Church of the Old Greyfriars, Edinburg. Though a difficult post of duty, he took rank as a pulpit orator of singular vigor and vivacity. It was not long before the church was crowded with hearers, many of them persons of high position and renown. But Dr. Guthrie had not occupied his church long before events occurred that led to a reform in the church over all Scotland. Up to this time he had been a firm believer in the Established Church as the church of all classes, rich and poor. So he was much annoyed by the notions of the Town Council increasing the seat rents, which meant exclusion of the poor. Continued and embarrassing interruptions on the part of the' State, in which the State interfered with the freedom and impaired the spirituality of the church, disregarding the rights of the people, led him, in the ultimate disruption which occurred, to cast his lot with the Free Church movement. With his congregation, he left St. John's Church, and found temporary accommodation in the Wesleyan Chapel in Nicolson Square. In a few years a new church was built for his congregation, close to the old one, in which he entered on a new era in his ministry, and was more popular and successful than ever.

Dr. Guthrie was a great orator; but he was something more. His ministry was fruitful in conversions, philanthropy, and reform.

Among his last utterances were these: "Affection is very sweet; and it is all one from whatever quarter it comes—whether from a Highland lassie or a peeress—just as to a thirsty man cold water is equally grateful from a spring on the hillside as from a richly ornamented fountain." On learning of the Queen's inquiry as to his condition, he said, "It is very kind," and parting with an humble servant he whispered, "God bless you, my *friend*."

JOSEPH PARKER, D. D.

In 1880, In Northumberland, England, Joseph Parker was born. It is a fact worth recording that the county where he had his birth has produced "such a lawyer as Lord Eldon, such an engineer as George Stephenson, and such a preacher as Thomas Binney."

Dr. Parker regards his training for the ministry as having begun at seven years of age. It might have begun much earlier than this, if it is true, as one has said that "to reform a man you must begin with his grandmother."

After a thorough training in the ancient languages and mathematics, he studied logic and philosophy in University College, London. For a short time he was the assistant of Dr. John Cambell, of the Whitefield Tabernacle, after which he settled at Banbury for five years, where he built a new chapel, only to leave it to succeed Dr. Robert Halley in Manchester, where he labored until 1869, when he was called to the Church in the Poultry, London,

He now began to become well-known to the public as preacher and author. By a Thursday morning series of discourses, he increased his congregation from the ranks of those who could not hear him on Sunday, He built the "City Temple,"a large structure at one end of Holborn viaduct, in the heart of the business portion of the metropolis. Here a large congregation gathers to listen to his ministrations, among which are many Americans. One cause of this is that Dr. Parker's published works are widely known on this side of the ocean; another is in the profound impression he produced by his magnificent address in Madison Avenue Presbyterian Church during the meeting of the Evangeal Alliance in New York in 1878.

His recent visit to America, to eulogise his friend Henry Ward Beecher, has increased our interest in him. His sermons, his lectures, notably the one on Gladstone, his addresses, but most of all the presence of *the man* have engaged the attention of the intelligent public. The writer has seen him, heard him. His is the eloquence of mighty thought. He is a. Voice, a Fire, a

Herald bold and eager in his sacred work, an orator in Heaven's name and strength. His friendly critics suggest that he should have been an actor; he is one. There is no broader sphere for legitimate oratorical action than the pulpit. In the modern church we have had no man who has done more in authorship to expound and interpret the hidden truth of Scripture than Joseph Parker. His "People's Bible" is a classic. His "Paraclete," "Ecce Homo," "Ecce Deus," "Ad Clerum" and "The Priesthood of Christ" are masterpieces. Among those of our century, whose lines have adorned the Christian Ministry, whose tongues have proclaimed the truth as it is in Christ, and whose pens have illustrated and made dear many of the "mysteries of the Book," the subject of this sketch is among the foremost.

ACCESS TO GOD

"For through Him we both have access by one Spirit unto the Father"—Eph. 3:18.

"Thou art the way:—to thee alone
From sin and death we flee;
And he who would the Father seek,
Must seek Him, Lord, by thee."
—GEORGE DOANE.

CHRIST THE ONLY MEANS

Ten thousand times the gate of Heaven has swung back and forth, but it never swings back and forth save as Christ opened it, and you will go in through Him or not at all. Christ wants you there. How do I know it? Suppose a man lost a diamond, and he looked for it eight or ten days, would you not conclude, from the fact that he looked for it so long, that he wanted the diamond? And when I find Christ seeking for your soul, seeking for it ever since it has been a soul, seeking for it by day and by night, seeking for it through heat and through cold, seeking for it with tears in His eyes, and blood on His brow, and scourges on His back, and a world of agony in His heart, I know that it is because He wants to find you. Oh, He has prepared a glorious Heaven for you! It is already waiting for you, not merely a throne, but steps by which to mount it. Not only a harp, but a tune to play on it. Not only a bannered procession, but a victory which it is to celebrate. God wants no vacant chairs at that banquet. He does not want those who stand around Him in glory to wonder why *you* have not been solicited. He does not want the Book of Life to thunder shut till your name is in it.—TALMAGE.

CHRIST THE ROAD

"I am the way." As a road is that along which men go to their daily avocations, God chooses it to represent Himself in this universal use, this underlying support of all things. Who would dare say this of God but God? Some beasts carry their young, and some birds carry their young, and mothers carry their children; but who but God would say, "I am the road; press me with your feet." This is the highway cast up; and on it the ransomed of the Lord shall return and come to Zion, with songs and everlasting joy upon their heads.—BEECHER.

CHRIST THE KEY

There are many locks in my house and all with different keys, but I have one master key which opens them all. So the Lord has many treasuries and secrets all shut up from carnal minds with locks which they cannot open; but he who walks in fellowship with Jesus possesses the master key, which will admit him to all the blessings of the covenant; yea, to the very heart of God. Through the Well-Beloved we have access to God, to Heaven, to every secret of the Lord.—SPURGEON.

CHRIST OUR CONQUEROR

It is said of Julian, the great apostate, that when he was trying to stamp out Christianity in the days of Rome's prosperity, before it received Christianity, when he was trying to drive those Christians away, he received a mortal wound, and as he pulled the spear out of his side, he took a handful of the blood that gushed forth from the wound, and as he threw it toward Heaven he reeled and staggered, crying out, "There, Galilean! Thou hast conquered." We are conquered, overcome by the blood of the Lamb. The only way to Heaven is by the word of His testimony and His blood. Every man that goes up, goes by way of the blood of Christ.—MOODY.

NONE BUT CHRIST

Till we are reconciled to God, and, born again through His Spirit, have become new creatures in Christ Jesus, we are His enemies. Our works do not spring from love for Him, and therefore cannot have any value in His eyes. And how imperfect are even the best works of the saints! There is foulness enough in the purest heart, and in respect of their motives, manner, and object, sin enough in our best actions—those whereby we do most good, and earn most commendation, to condemn us. To speak of us not in our worst, but in our best state, not of the sins we commit, but of the services we render, our wine has its water, our silver has its dross. And so, abandoning every hope of acceptance with a holy God through our own merit, let us cling to Christ, as a drowning man to the plank that, embraced in his arms, floats him to shore; the language of our faith an echo of His who breathed out His life with these words on His lips, "None but Christ I none but Christ."—GUTHRIE.

ACTIVITY

"Whatsoever thy hand findeth to do, do it with thy might; for there is no work, nor device, nor knowledge, nor wisdom, in the grave, whither thou goest."—Eccles. 9:10.

> Hark the voice of Jesus calling,
> "Who will go and work to-day?
> Fields are white and harvests waiting,
> Who will bear the sheaves away?"
> Loud and long the master calleth,
> Rich reward He off era free;
> Who will answer, gladly saying,
> "Here am I, send me, send me?"
> —DANIEL MARCH.

A MEANS OF GRACE

Religion has been brought into the sphere of ordinary and practical things, and made to consist in the right ordering of disposition and conduct in the usual duties of life.

The great duties of life as they are ordinarily distributed, both in the household and out of it, are indispensable to the development of the whole nature of man, and of the prime virtues; and they are the instruments, or, to employ the language of ancient times, the "means of grace," in life. The church, the lecture room, the prayer and conference meeting, the communion of saints, were once spoken of as "means of grace." They are means of grace when they produce grace; but it would seem, in the very use of them, as if they were meant to exclude common life, common duties, common occupations; whereas, in the divine economy, everything which pertains to the well-being of the individual, and the prosperity of the household, and the welfare of the community in which men live, tends to that amassing of force which results in civilization. Everything which occupies thought, and ripens into enterprise, and ripens enterprise into success and fruitful achievement, is part and parcel of the divine scheme.

Therefore the man who bends over his bench may be as really worshiping God, fulfilling the will of God, and doing God's service as he who reads from the Psalms or the Gospels. He who is rightly performing the duties of life is worshiping, if worship means rendering acceptable service to God.

One who gives the full activity of his nature to the things which concern him in the sphere where God has planted him, has his mind in that condition which it will ever be in communion with God. Activity in business gives that vitality, that wholesome, fresh condition of mind, which is the very prime ingredient of fervency of spirit; and this fervency, this life which is produced by force, is to a very large extent the source of our strength; the source of our good moral judgment; the source of all those virtues which are to be developed in us.—BEECHER.

AN AID TO COURAGE

Courage maintains itself by its ardent action, as some birds rest on the wing. There is an energy about agility that will often give a man a fortitude which otherwise he might not have possessed. We can picture the gallant regiment at Balaclava riding into the valley of death at a dashing gallop, but we could scarcely imagine their marching slowly up to the guns, coolly calculating the deadly odds of the adventure.

There is much in our obeying as our Lord did, "straight-way."

When the Lord gives his servants grace to follow out their convictions as soon as they feel them, then they act courageously. First thoughts are best in the service ef God, they are like Gideon's men that lapped. Second thoughts come up timorously and limpingly, and incite us to make provision for the flesh, like those men whom Gideon discarded because they went down on their knees to drink, taking things too leisurely to be fit for the Lord's battles.—SPURGEON.

A LAW OF GOD

No one who has read the Scripture will say that it does not teach us to work. Every Bible student loves to work. The Word of God inspires us to work. Paul said the love of Christ constrained him. Jeremiah said the Word of God burned in his bones. He fed upon it and it was sweet to his taste. If a man gets his heart full of the Word of God, he is not then interested just in one little corner of the vineyard, but he will take a wide field of labor and interest.

The first words that fell from the lips of Christ on earth, so far as we have them on record, were, "Wist ye not that I must be about my Father's business?" You will find that during His ministry, He toiled early and late in the work. After we are saved we cannot help going to work. If a man tells me he has been saved of Christ, and yet has no desire to work for God, I know it is a spurious conversion; it is not a true salvation; it has not the ring of Heaven in it—MOODY.

ACTIVITY BETOKENS LIFE

There may be the appearance of life, but certainly not its presence, where there is no activity; as they rightly concluded, who, sailing in Arctic seas, fell in with a ship for long years imprisoned in the ice, and looked in its cabin on a strange, appalling, wierd-like scene. Fifty years had come and gone since living voice or step had sounded there, yet there were all the crew. They lay in couches on the floor, each attired in the dress and presenting the form and flesh of life; while their captain sat by the cabin table, pen in hand, and the log spread out before him. The spectators of so strange a sight, with mingled feelings of doubt and terror, shouted; but no response came back. Nor crew nor captain stirred. All were dead, and had been corpses for half a century—the frosts that killed preserving them. Life-like as he looked who bent over the table with a pen in his fingers and paper before him, in which, the last survivor, he had recorded their sufferings, he also was dead; as they knew on seeing him sit unmoved by their shouts; his eyes retaining their glassy stare, and his form its fixed and frozen posture. The activity that thus marks all other kinds of life, is characteristic of the Christian's. Sometimes distinguished by heroic daring, and prodigal of noble deeds, at all times, it is a life of doing.—GUTHRIE.

You will get out of this world just so much as, under God, you earn by your own hand and brain. Horatius was told that he might have so much land as he could plow around in one day with a yoke of oxen, and I have noticed that men get nothing in this world, that is worth possessing, of a financial, moral, or spiritual nature, save as they get it by their own hard work. It is just so much as, from the morning to the evening of your life, you can plow around by your own continuous and hard-sweating activity." —TALMAGE.

ADOPTION

"For ye have not received the spirit of bondage again to fear, but ye have received the Spirit of adoption, whereby we cry, Abba, Father."—Rom. 8:15.

"I once was an outcast stranger on earth,
 A sinner by choice, and an alien by birth;
But I've been adopted, my name's written down,
 An heir to a mansion, a robe and a crown."
  —HATTIE E. BUELL.

GOD'S FATHERHOOD NOT COMPREHENDED

"A young child does not know his father's strength. We are weak creatures, and cannot conceive fully of the perfections of God; we know not what the power of God can do for us. It would be the height of absurdity for the child to think and speak of his father as if he were a child too, and could do no more than the boy's playmates. Yet this is the common error of the children of God. We do not raise our thoughts to a God-like level. We think our own thoughts of God, and straightway we doubt. Oh that we rose to God's thoughts, and tried to conceive how He looks upon matters! Surely He taketh up the isles as a very little thing, and the mountains He weighs in scales.

If our troubles were set in the light of God's power, and love, and faithfulness, and wisdom, they would become to us small burdens; why should we not so regard them? Why must we reckon as children? Why not compute our load by our Father's measurement, and then see how easily it will be carried? Estimating divine strength by human standards is one of the childish things which we must put away.

O Father, forgive me for having so often limited Thee, and teach me never again to judge after the flesh."— SPURGEON.

GOD'S PLAN FOR MAN'S HAPPINESS

"T"is ill-proportioned theology that teaches the doctrine, that the only motive in redemption was a regard to God's glory. It receives no countenance from the Bible. Does not God "pity us, as a father pitieth his children?". Taught to address him by the endearing appellation of Father, oh, what affection, love, and loving-kindness are expressed in that tender term! And if, on seeing some earthly father, whom a child's scream has reached and roused, rush up the blazing stairs, or leap into the boiling flood, it were wrong, it were cruel, it were a shame, to suspect him of being destitute of affection—of being moved to this noble act by no other motive than a regard to his own honor, and by no other voice than the calm command of duty—how much more wrong were it to harbor such suspicions of "our Father who is in heaven."—GUTHRIE.

THE WANDERER RECEIVED

Perhaps there is no subject in the Bible that takes hold of me with as great force as this subject of the wandering child. It enters deeply into my own life; it comes right home into our own family. The first thing I remember was the death of my father, I remember nothing about the funeral, but his death has made a lasting impression upon me. After my mother's subsequent sickness, my eldest brother to whom mother looked up to comfort her in her loneliness, and in her great affliction, became a wanderer; he left home. I need not tell you how that mother mourned for her boy, how she waited day by day and month by month for his return. I need not say how night after night she watched, and wept, and prayed. Many a time we were told to go to the post-office to see if a letter had not come from him, but we had to bring back the sorrowful words, "No letter yet, mother." Many a time as I walked up to the house, I have heard my mother pray, "O God, bring back my boy." Many a time did she lift her heart up to God in prayer for her boy. When the wintry gale would blow around the house, and the gale would rage without, her dear face would wear a terribly anxious look, and she would utter in piteous tones, "Oh, my dear boy; perhaps he is on the ocean this fearful night. O God, preserve him!" We would sit around the fireside of an evening and ask her to tell us about our father, and she would talk for hours about him; but if the mention of my eldest brother should chance to come in, then all would be hushed; she never spoke of him but with tears. Many a time did she try to conceal them, but all was in vain, and when Thanksgiving day came, a chair was set for him. Our friends and neighbors gave him up, but mother had faith that she would see him again. One day in the middle of summer, a stranger was seen approaching the house. He came up on the east piazza and looked upon my mother through the window. The man had a long beard, and when mother first saw him, she did not start or rise, but when she saw the great tears trickling down his cheeks, she cried, "It's my boy, my dear, dear boy," and sprang to the window. But there the boy stood, and said, "Mother, I will never cross the treshhold until you say you forgive me." Do you think he had to stay there long? No, no, her arms were soon around him, and she wept upon his shoulder as did the father of the prodigal son when he returned home. I heard of it when in a distant city, and what a thrill of joy shot through me! But what joy on earth can equal the joy in heaven when a wandering child comes home? The matchless parable of the Prodigal was recorded solely to show us the love and compassion of God who waits to receive into the relation of sonship every wandering soul.—MOODY.

GOD INVITES US

"You know how rapidly the snow-flakes can accumulate on a winter's day, and you know how soon they aggregate on the top of the Alps; and then, in certain conditions of the weather, that great block of snow which is made up of little snowflakes shoves off an avalanche on the villages beneath, destroying them. So the sins of your life—cold, freezing transgressions—accumulating, accumulating, heaping up wrath against the day of wrath, at last, if unrepented of, will be an avalanche of darkness rolling down upon your soul. They seem more like a cloud, black, thunder-charged, and flash with all the lightning of an incensed God, and then hover and swing about us until in the suffocation we gasp for mercy, and hope that a gale from heaven will blow away the cloud. God is willing to lift that cloud. He says he is long-suffering and patient. He is the God of great pity. He is willing to blot out all your transgressions. He is willing to take you in the arms of His compassion. Oh, here is the letter! It is a letter from your Father, offended and outraged. It is a letter to you, the straying child. He says "Come back, come back! Though your sins were as scarlet, they shall be as snow; though they be red like crimson, they shall be as wool." Pardon for all! Free pardon!

Everlasting pardon! Adoption! Sonship! Oh, child, come home to Father, your Father, home, your home."—TALMAGE.

THE PRICE OF CHRIST'S DEPARTURE

Christ said that it was expedient that he should go away, because if he did not go the Comforter would not come. The Spirit; the Holy Spirit; the one who stands over against those subtle elements in the human soul which we call the spiritual instinct or sentiment—this Holy Spirit comes to take the place of Christ, and crown us sons in the kingdom of Cod. This is infinitely better than that Christ had continued on the earth in his physical form. O throne of Grace were He sits regnant who is my Brother! O Jesus, crowned, not for thine own glory, but with power of love for our struggling spirits, Thou art my Christ—my Brother—My Father's Son!—BEECHER.

AFFLICTION

"For our light affliction, which is but for a moment, worketh out for us a far more exceeding and eternal weight of glory"— 2 Cor. 4:17.

"Go then, earthly fame and treasure!
  Come, disaster, scorn and pain!
In Thy service, pain is pleasure;
  With Thy favor loss is gain.
"Man may trouble and distress me,
  'Twill but drive me to Thy breast;
Life with trials hard may press me,
  Heaven will bring me sweeter rest."
      —HENRY F. LYTE.

AFFLICTION CEMENTS HEARTS

Afflictions make friendships. There was an Englishman in Chicago the winter before the fire, who was much impressed with the rapid growth of the city. He went back to Manchester where he told the people about the city only forty years old, with all its fine buildings, its colleges, its churches. He thought it was a most wonderful city. But no one seemed to take any interest in Chicago. "But,"Tie says, "one day the news came flashing over the wires that Chicago was burning. Then they suddenly became interested about Chicago. Every man I had told about Chicago became interested, and couldn't hear too much. The news came flashing under the sea that half the city was burnt. There were men who couldn't help but weep." At last the news came that 100,000 people were homeless, and were in danger of starvation, unless immediate help was sent. Then these men came forward and gave their thousands. It was the calamity that visited Chicago that brought out the love and pity of those men.— MOODY.

A DELIVERER

Is it dark with thee, my friend? It has been quite as dark with myself, and yet I have seen light descending on the rugged hills and making those hills as steps up to heaven. Art thou afraid of the coming days, lest they bring with them edged weapons, pain, grief, loss, friendliness, and desolation? Put thy hand into the palm wounded for thee, the palm of the one Infinite Savior. He knows all—He is the treasurer of the future—the great dragon is tamed by the anger of His eye—and they who trust Him with all their love, shall be set amidst the safety, the peace, and the glory of His eternal Zion.—PARKER.

AFFLICTIONS DO NOT ENTIRELY CRUSH THE HEART

"I have seen the characters of the writing remain on paper that the flames had turned into a film of buoyant coal; I have seen the thread that had passed through the fire retain, in the cold gray ashes, the twist it had got in spinning; I have found every shivered splinter of the flint as hard as the unbroken stone; and, let trials come, in providence, sharp as the fire, and ponderous as the crushing hammer, unless God send with these something else than these, bruised, broken, bleeding as the heart may be, it remains the same."—GUTHRIE.

NO LIFE EXEMPT

Trouble is an apothecary that mixes a great many draughts, bitter and sour, and nauseous, and you must drink some one of them. Trouble puts up a great many packs, and you must carry some of.them. There is no sandal so thick and well adjusted but some thorn will strike through it. There is no sound so sweet, but the undertaker's screw-driver grates through it. In this swift shuttle of the heart some of the threads must break.

We pluck some of our best comforts from the very midst of our trials. I have noticed that some of the sweetest berries grow on the sharpest thorns.

Afflictions are loathsome things, but they are necessary. They are leeches that draw out the inflammation of the soul.—TALMAGE.

AFFLICTIONS GOD'S MERCIES

God washes the eyes by tears until they can behold the otherwise invisible land where tears shall come no more. O, Love! O, Affliction! Ye are the guides that show us the way through the great airy space where our loved ones walked; and as hounds easily follow the scent before the dew be risen, so God teaches us, while our sorrow is tear-wet to follow on and find our dear ones in Heaven.— BEECHER.

ATONEMENT

"He was wounded for our transgressions, He was bruised for our iniquities. The chastisement of our peace was upon Him; and with His stripes we are healed. All we like sheep have gone astray; we have turned every one to his own way; and the Lord hath laid on Him the iniquity of us all."—Isaiah 53:5.

> "Hail to the Lord's anointed,
>   Great David's greater Son!
> Hail in the time appointed,
>   His reign on earth begun l
> He comes to break oppression,
>   To set the captive free;
> To take away transgression,
>   And rule in equity.
>   —JAMES MONTGOMERY.

GOD'S GREATEST WORK

Of all God's works, redemption through His Son's atonement is the greatest; it is His "strange" work. That cross on Calvary, which mercy raised for you, cost more love, and labor, and wisdom, and skill, than all yon starry universe. With the earth its emerald floor, its roof the sapphire firmament, the sun and stars its pendant lamps, its incense a thousand fragrant odors, its music of many sounds and instruments, the song of groves, the murmur of the streams, the voice of winged winds, the pealing thunder, and the everlasting roar of ocean, nature's is a glorious temple! Yet that is a nobler temple, which, with blood-redeemed saints for its living stones, and God and the Lamb for its uncreated lights, stands aloft on the Rock of Ages—the admiration of angels, and the glory of the universe.—GUTHRIE.

THE ATONEMENT COMPLETE

Two relationships made Jesus' atonement successful. He was human, and therefore on our side. He was Divine, and therefore on God's side. A righteous decree had gone forth, that because of their sins, a race must die. Jesus said, "That shall not be. I am God. I belong to God. I belong to the race. I will take these two relationships into the negotiation. I will redeem mankind, though it cost my life." "O, stop!" cried all the hosts of heaven. "Your blood will redden the door-steps of the world. You will only be sacrificed." "No," says Christ, "I will not stop. I know all the torment; I know all the bleeding; I know the death that is to come; but I willingly throw myself across the sharp edges of this undertaking. Stand back, men, angels, and devils, I come to the rescue. God must be reconciled. The decree must be revoked. Here I drop into the tortures and massacre. If I perish, I perish."

Wonder of wonders! Jesus, with the tears of human sorrow in one hand, and the key of eternal domination in the other, appears to put away our sin by the sacrifice of Himself.—TALMAGE.

A PROOF OF DIVINE TENDERNESS

God showed His love for us in that He died for us while we were yet enemies. He showed His love for us in that He suffered for our sake. God bears us as sick babes are borne in the arms of nurses through all the years of our life. And when at last we come to the gate of heaven, we are none of us to enter into the land of the blest because we can say, "Behold I am accordant, symmetric, perfected!" None of us are to go into the heavenly land by reason of the many good deeds we have performed. Every one of us, entering in, will say, "I am borne by the motherhood and fatherhood of God, who has taken pity on me in my distress; and I am what I am by the wonderous love and care of God. Open, ye gates, that I may see Him who loved me, and died for me! Open, ye long ranks between me and my God, that I may behold that love and salvation which has by its virtue and power, drawn men upward, as the sun draws flowers from the soil. I shall go into heaven as one redeemed by the love of God, the atonement of Christ, and the ministrations of the Holy Spirit.—BEECHER.

WE DO NOT APPRECIATE IT

If a prince, passing by an execution, should take the malefactor's chains, and suffer in his stead, the deed would ring through all history, and be quoted as an amazing instance of heroic pity; and well deserved would be all the words of praise and sonnets of admiration which would record and eulogize it. Yet, our Lord Jesus did this, and infinitely more for those who were not merely malefactors but enemies to His own throne and person. This is a wonder of wonders! But it meets with small praise. The most of men around us have heard of it, and treated it as of little import; as an idle tale; as a pious legend; as a venerable fable; as an unpractical myth. Even those who know, believe, and admire, are cold in their emotions with regard to the story of the atonement. Herein is love which ought to set our hearts on fire, and yet we scarcely maintain a smoldering spark of enthusiasm. Lord Jesus, be more real to our apprehensions, and more completely the master of our affections.—SPURGEON.

THE GOSPEL MESSAGE

I was in a city in Europe, and a young minister came to me and said, "Moody, what makes the difference be-tween your preaching and mine? Either you are right, and I am wrong, or you are wrong, and I am right." Said I, "I don't know what the difference is, for you have heard me, and I have never heard you preach. What is the difference?" Said he, "You make a great deal of the death of Christ, and I don't make anything out of it. I don't think it has anything to do with it. I preach the life." Said I, "What do you do with this: 'He hath borne our sins in His own body on the tree?'" Said he, "I never preached that." Said I, "What do you do with this: 'He was wounded for our transgressions; He was bruised for our iniquities, and with His stripes we are healed?'" Said he, "I never preached that." "Well," said I again, "What do you do with this: 'Without the shedding of blood there is no remission?'" Said he, "I never preached that." I asked him, "What do you preach?" "Well," he says, "I preach a moral essay." Said I, "My friend, if you take the atoning blood out of the Bible, it is all a myth to me." Said he, "I think the whole thing is a sham." "Then," said I, "I advise you to get out of the ministry very quick. I would not preach a sham. If the Bible is untrue, let us stop preaching, and come out at once like men, and fight against it; but if these things are true, and Jesus Christ left heaven and came into this world to shed His blood and thereby save sinners, then let us lay hold of it and preach it in season and out of season." In the seminary at Princeton, last year, when the students were ready to graduate, the old man, their instructor stood up before them, and said, "Young men, make much of the blood. Young men, make much of the blood!" And I have learned this, that a minister who makes much of the blood, of the atonement, of substitution, and holds Christ up as the sinner's only hope, God blesses his preaching. And if the Apostles did not preach that, what did they preach?—MOODY.

THE BIBLE

"Thy word is truth." John 17:17. "The word of our God shall stand forever." Isaiah 40:8.

"Within this ample volume lies
    The mystery of mysteries.
Happiest they of human race,
    To whom their God has given Grace
To read, to fear, to hope, to pray,
    To lift the latch, to force the way;
And better had they ne'er been born,
    That read to doubt, or read to scorn."
              —SIR WALTER SCOTT.

WORTHY OF STUDY

    I know that young doctors, young lawyers, young accountants, young mechanics, young merchants, have but little time for general reading. If so, then spend more of that time at the fountain of divine truth from which nearly all the books have been dipped that are worth anything. I will undertake to say that every great book, that has been published since the first printing press was lifted, has directly or indirectly derived much of its power from the sacred oracles. Goethe, the admired of all skeptics, had the wall of his home at Wiemar covered with religious maps and pictures. Milton's "Paradise Lost" is part of the Bible in blank verse. Tasso's "Jerusalem Delivered" is borrowed from the Bible. Spencer's writings are imitations of the parables. John Bunyan saw in a dream only what St. John had seen before in Apocalyptic vision. Macaulay crowns his most gigantic sentences with Scripture quotations. Through Addison's "Spectator" there glances in and out the stream that broke from beneath the throne of God, clear as crystal. Walter Scott's characters are Bible men and women under different names. Meg Merribes, the witch of Endor. Shakespeare's Lady Macbeth was Jezebel. Hobbes stole from this "Castle of Truth" the weapons with which he afterward assaulted it. Lord Byron caught the ruggedness and majesty of his style from the prophecies. The writings of Pope are saturated with Isaiah, and he finds his most successful theme in the Messiah. The poets Thompson and Johnson, dipped their pens in the style of the inspired orientals. Thomas Carlyle is only a splendid distortion of Ezekiel; and wandering through the lanes and parks of this imperial domain of Bible truth, I find all the great American, English, German, Spanish, Italian poets, painters, orators, and rhetoricians. Now if this be so, and the young man has but little time to read, why not go to the great fountain of all truth and inspiration, from which these other books dip their life.---TALMAGE.

LIKE HIDDEN GOLD

The truths of the Bible are like gold in the soil. Whole generations walk over it, and know not what treasures are hidden beneath. So centuries of men pass over the Scriptures, and know not what riches lie under the feet of their interpretation. Sometimes when they discover them, they call them new truths. One might as well call gold, newly dug, new gold.

The Bible, without a spiritual life to interpret it, is like a trellis on which no vine grows—bare, angular and in the way. The Bible with a spiritual life, is like a trellis covered with a luxuriant vine—beautiful, odorous, and heavy with purple clusters shining through the leaves.—BEECHER.

A PEOPLE'S BOOK

More Bible is what is needed. The Bible must be taken out of the hands of the priest, and put into the hands of the people. I will not have it that the Bible is a mystery in the sense of being accessible only by experts; it is the people's book in the sense that the air is the people's air, and the firmament is the people's firmament. Of course the scientific man has his own view of the sky, and his own way of examining the air, yet the poorest dunce may look up into the solemn heights, and the meanest drudge drink in the living air. Many people could make more of the sky itself than of a learned lecture upon it, and a mountain breeze could be appreciated when a chemical analysis would be misunderstood. It is so with the Bible. Let the people themselves read "Moses and the prophets," not send for a priest to read for them, but sit down to the sacred task and spell out the infinite thoughts.—PARKER.

ITS PRECIOUS VALUE

There is gold in the rocks which fringe the Pass of the Splugen, gold even in the stones which mend the roads, but there is too little of it to be worth extracting. Alas, how like too many books and sermons! Not so the Scripture; they are much fine gold; their very dust is precious.

Let no one turn away from the Bible because it is not a book of learning and wisdom. It is, would ye know astronomy? It is here; it tells you of the Sun of Righteousness and the Star of Bethlehem. Would you know Botany? It is here; it tells you of the plant of renown— the "Lily of the Valley," and the "Rose of Sharon." Would you know geology and minerology? You shall learn it here; for you may read of the Rock of Ages, and the White Stone with the name graven thereon, which no man knoweth save he that receiveth it. Would ye study history? Here is the most ancient of all the records of the history of the human race. Whate'er your science is, come and bend over this book, your science is here.—SPURGEON.

AN INTERESTING BOOK

We want to bear in mind that the Bible is not a dry uninteresting book, as a great many skeptics try to make out. They say, "We want something new; we have out-grown that." Why, the word of God is the only new book in the world. All that the newspapers can do is to tell of things as they have taken place, but the Bible tells of things that will take place. We do not consider the Bible enough as a whole. We just take up a word here and a word there, a verse here and a verse there, a chapter here and a chapter there, and not in a systematic way. We therefore know very little about the Bible. I will guarantee that the majority of Christians in America only read the Bible at family worship; and you will notice too, that they have to put a bookmark in to tell where they left off the day before. Ask them an hour after, what they have read, and they have forgotten all about it. Of course we cannot get much knowledge of the Bible in that way. When I was a boy I worked on a farm and I hoed corn so poorly that when I left off, I had to take a stick and mark the place, so I could tell the next morning where I had stopped the night before. If I didn't I would likely as not hoe the same row over again.

In order to understand the Bible we will have to study it carefully.—MOODY.

ITS SUFFICIENCY

Within the two boards of the poor man's Bible is a greater wealth of happiness, of honor, of pleasure, of true peace, than Australia hides in the gold of all her mines. That, for example, could not buy the pardon of any of the thousand criminals of a country, which, weary of their crimes, once cast on her distant shores; but here is what satisfies a justice stricter than man's and procures the forgiveness of sins of which the stoutest heart may tremble to think.—GUTHRIE.

THE BLOOD OF JESUS

"If we walk in the light as He is in the light, we have fellowship one with another, and the blood of Jesus Christ His Son cleanseth us from all sin."—1 John 1:7.

"Hail, thou once despised Jesus!
Hail, thou Galilean King!
Thou didst suffer to release us.
Thou didst free salvation bring.
Hail, thou agonizing Savior,
Bearer of our sin and shame!
By Thy merits we find favor;
Life is given through Thy name."
—JOHN BAKEWELL.

HIS BLOOD MAKES ALL MEN BROTHERS

The blood of Jesus Christ makes all nations akin. Then look not for your relations in your own house or in your own sphere. Christ's blood is stronger for relationship than blood of father or mother. Look above you. All there are yours. Go down to the bottom of society. All below you are judgment-day, brothers; God's eternity is on them and you alike.—BEECHER.

The blood of the atoning God is the life fluid of Mis church. Spilt on Calvary, it has nourished into richness the tree on which a Savior suffered, and no longer is it bare and naked, but a foliage-laden forest of shelter-growing branches.—CHARLES B. MANLY.

THE OBJECT OF OUR FAITH

Is thy faith fixed on the precious blood? Then thou art in the covenant. Canst thou read thy name in the bloody characters of a Savior's atonement, who says to all "Come unto me?" Then shalt thou read it one day in the golden letters of the Father's election. He that believeth is elected. The blood is the symbol, the token, the earnest, the surety, the seal of the covenant of grace to thee. By this blood, sin is cancelled; by Jesus' agonies, justice is satisfied; by His death, the law is honored; and by that blood in all its mediatorial efficacy, and in all its cleansing power, Christ fulfills all that He stipulated to do on the behalf of His people towards God.—SPURGEON.

THE ONLY GOSPEL—THAT OF HIS BLOOD

Be assured that any religion which makes light of the blood is of its father, the devil. No matter how eloquent a man is, if he preaches against the blood he is doing the devil's work. Do not listen to him. Do not believe him. If an angel from heaven should preach any other gospel, I would not believe it. "Christ's blood shed for the pardon of our sins,"—that is the gospel that Paul preached, and Peter preached, and that God has always honored in the salvation of men's souls.—MOODY.

OUR RANSOM

To save us from sin, and from that hell where they seek for death but cannot find it, and only find after unnumbered ages that their torments are beginning. Jesus interposed, saying, "I will save them—suspend the sentence— I come to do thy will, O, my God, deliver from going down to the pit, I have found a ransom—have patience with them and I will pay thee all!" He paid it. Making atonement for sin "He was wounded for our transgressions; he was bruised for our iniquities; the chastisement of our peace was upon Him; and with his stripes we are healed." The debt was paid on Calvary to the uttermost farthing; and now God only awakens our convictions and alarms our consciences, reckoning with us, that He may bring sinners to acknowledge their guilt, and so prepare them to receive His mercy.—GUTHRIE.

THE BLOOD OF A KING

A king dying! You remember when the last Czar of Russia was in his fatal sickness, that bulletins were every hour dispatched from the palace, saying,

"The king is better," or "The king is worse," or "The king is delirious," or "The king rested easier through the night," or "The king is dying," or "The king is dead." The bells tolled it, the flag signaled it, the telegraphs flashed it. Tell it now to all the earth and to all the heavens—Jesus, our King, is sick with His last sickness. Let couriers carry the swift dispatch. His pains are worse. He is breathing a last groan; through His body quivers the last anguish; the King is dying; THE KING IS DEAD! Ye who come round about the cross, look what is beneath. It is royal blood.—TALMAGE.

BROTHERLY LOVE

"Let brotherly love continue."—Heb. 13:1.

"There are lonely hearts to cherish,
    While the days are going by;
There are weary souls who perish,
    While the days are going by.
If a smile we can renew,
    As our journey we pursue—
O the good we all may do,
    While the days are going by."

PROMPTED BY COMPASSION

The story goes that Henry the Eighth, wandering one night in the streets of London in disguise, was met at the bridge foot by some of the watch, and not giving a good account of himself was carried off to the Poultry Compter, and shut up for the night without fire or candle. On his liberation, he made a grant of thirty chaldrons of coals and a quantity of bread for the solace of night prisoners in the Compter. Experience brings brotherly love. Those who have felt sharp afflictions, terrible convictions, racking doubts and violent temptations, will be jealous in helping those of a similar condition. It were well if the great Head of the church would put unsympathetic Christians into the Compter of trouble for a season until they can weep with those that weep.—SPURGEON.

SHAM LOVE

There is a good deal of what we might call sham love. People profess to love you very much, when you find it is all on the surface. It is not heart love. Very often you are in a person's house, and the servant comes in and says such a person is in the front room, and she says, "Oh, dear, I am so sorry he has come, I can't bear the sight of him and she'll get right up and go into the other room and say, "Why, how do you do? I am so glad to see you." There is a good deal of that sort of thing in the world. I remember I was talking with a man one day, and an acquaintance of his came in, and he jumped up at once and shook him by the hand—I thought he was going to shake his hand out of joint, he shook so hard,—and he seemed to be so glad to see him, and wanted him to stay, but the man was in a great hurry, and could not stay, and he coaxed and urged him to stay, but the man said no, he would come at another time; and after that man went out, my companion turned to me and said, u Well, he is an awful bore, and I'm glad he's gone." Well I began to feel that I was a bore too, and so I got out as quick as I could. That is not real love. That is love with the tongue, while the heart is not true. Now let us not love in word and in tongue, but in deed and in truth. That is the kind of love God gives us.—MOODY.

AN EXAMPLE OF LOVE

On the deck of a foundering vessel stood a negro slave. The last man left on board, he was about to step into the lifeboat. She was almost laden to the gunwale, to the water's edge. Bearing in his arms what seemed a heavy bundle, the boats crew who with difficulty kept her afloat in the roaring sea, refused to receive him. If he came it must be unincumbered and alone, on that they insisted. He must either leave that bundle and leap in, or throw it in and stay to perish. Pressing it to his bosom, he opened its folds; and there, warmly wrapped, lay two little children, whom their father had committed to his care. He kissed them and bade the sailors carry his affectionate farewell to his master, telling him how faithfully he had fulfilled his charge. Then lowering the children into the boat, which pushed off, the dark man stood alone on the deck, to go down with the sinking ship, a noble example of bravery, and true fidelity, and the "love that seeketh not its own."

BROTHERLY LOVE MEANS LOVE TO ALL

If any man's sorrows need our sympathy, his bodily or spiritual wants our help, let us think no more of asking whether he belongs to our country or family, our party or church, than if we saw him stretching out his hands from the window of a burning house, or found him, like the object of the

Samaritan's kindness, wallowing in a pool of blood. Thus Christ loved us; and thus he teaches us to love one another.—GUTHRIE.

THE BEAUTY OF LOVE

Oh, there is something beautiful in sympathy, in love, in manly, wifely, motherly, yea and neighborly love. Why was it that our city was aroused with excitement last week when a little child was kidnapped from one of our streets? Why where whole columns of newspapers filled with the story of a little child. It was because we are all one in love, and every parent said: "How if it had been my Lizzie? how if it had been my Mary? how if it had been my Maud? how if it had been my child? how if there had been one unoccupied pillow in our trundle bed tonight? how if my little one, bone to my bone, and flesh of my flesh, were to-night carried captive into some den of vagabonds, never to come back to me? how if it had been my sorrow looking out of the window, watching and waiting, that sorrow worse than death?" Then when they found her, why did we declare the news all through the households, and everybody that knew how to pray said: "Thank God!" Because we are all one, bound by one great golden chain of love.—TALMAGE.

LOVE—WHAT IT IS

Love is not mere good nature. We speak of the duty of all men to be loving in disposition; to be the incarnation of love as nearly as may be; and one says "That is my doctrine. I do not believe in those always dry, metaphysical men, arguing, and arguing, and arguing." Another man says, "That is my idea about it. I do not like those men who arc always combative. I like a mild, meek, and lowly man." I do not mean any such thing as that. I do not mean those lazy, sunshiny, good-natured men, who have no particular opinions, and who would about as soon have things go one way as another; who are without sharp and discriminating thought, have no preferences, no indignation, no conscience, no fire. I do not believe in any such men. I like to see a man who has got snap in every part of him, who knows how to think and to speak, and to put on the screw, if that is his particular mode of working.

This sweet heart quality I am speaking of, is the atmosphere in which every other faculty works. Do you suppose that love has no anger? There is no such anger as that which love furnishes. Do you suppose that when a mother sees the child, that is both herself and him whom she loves better than herself, the child in whom her hope is bound up, the child that is God's glass through which she sees immortality, the child that is more to her than her own life, doing a detestable meanness, that she is not angry and indignant, and that the child does not feel the smart of physical advice? You might as well say the summer shower has no thunder, as to say that love has no anger. —BEECHER.

CHARITY

"And now abideth faith, hope, charity, these three; but the greatest of these is charity."—1 Cor. 13:13.

"Lord, lead the way the Savior went,
By lane and cell obscure,
And let love's treasures still be spent,
Like His, upon the poor.
—WILLIAM CROSWELL.

A PLEA FOR GREATER LIBERALITY

Instead of cutting down the support of those missionaries in foreign lands, I think it would be better for us to cut off some of our luxuries. When a man can drive out with a four in-hand, let him give up two of his horses, and give what he saves by it to the foreign mission field. He could enjoy his religion better. People say that such a man died worth so many millions. It does not make any difference how much a man accumulates, he can't die worth anything. He isn't worth a penny; and so if you want to save money, lay it up in heaven. Make yourself rich by investing in good, institutions, and maintaining good works. I want to be rich for eternity, not for time. —MOODY.

OPPORTUNITIES FOR EXERCISING CHARITY

None of us liveth to himself; no man or woman should. Yet in this country what an immense amount of power is lost—lost to God, and to the world! I know a person in an humble position—she is a blacksmith's wife—who, sparing some hours each day for the work, has educated not a few of the neglected children where she resides. Her name though unknown to fame, is known to heaven; and, better than on gold or marble is graven on loving hearts. How many woman there are, who, treading in her humble footsteps, could change a languid into a bright, happy blessed life! In this world of sin and misery, time ought not to be wasted on trifles; well-spent hours, like drops of oil spreading on the waters diffuse themselves in blessing and pleasure all the day.—GUTHRIE.

THE RESULT OF CHARITY IN MISSIONS

Here is a man who gives a thousand dollars to the missionary cause. Men cry out, "What a waste! what's the use of sending New Testaments and missionaries, and spending your money in that way? Why don't you send plows, and corn threshers, and locomotives, and telegraphs!" But is it a waste? Ask the nations that have been saved; "Have not religious always preceded financial blessings?" Show me a nation where the Gospel of Christ triumphs, and I will show you a community prospered in a worldly sense. It is a waste to comfort the distressed, to instruct the ignorant, to back the immoral, to capture for God the innumerable hosts of men who erst with quick feet were tramping the way to hell? Alas! for the man who has nothing better than "greenbacks" and Government securities! There is no safe investment save that which is made in the bank, of which God holds the keys.—TALMAGE.

THE RIGHT MOTIVE

To be praised, and to have the reputation of liberality, is the way many people have of taking interest in what they lend to the Lord. It is probable that benevolence is only the cat's paw of vanity, when our obscure and casual kindness seem to us like pale, inodorous flowers grown in a solitary wood, and only public charities have color and fragrance. A man should fear when he only enjoys what good he does publicly. Is it not the publicity rather than the charity he loves? Is it not vanity, rather than benevolence, that gives such charities? A man must be very rich in secret charities before he can bear the strain of public beneficence.—BEECHER.

TRUE CHARITY

If men valued the truth as they do their goods and their houses, they would not regard error with such cool contentment. The cant of the present day cries "Charity, Charity." As if it were not the truest charity to grow indignant with that which ruins souls. It is not uncharitable to warn men against poisonous adulterations of their food, or invasion of their rights; and surely it can not be more uncharitable to put them upon their guard against that which will poison or rob their souls.—SPURGEON.

CHEERFULNESS

"Rejoice in the Lord alway; and again I say rejoice."— *Phil. 4:4.*

"Let us gather up the sunbeams,
   Lying all around our path;
Let us keep the wheat and roses,
   Casting out the thorns and chaff.
Let us find our sweetest comfort
   In the blessings of to-day,
With a patient hand removing
   All the briars from the way."

CHEERFULNESS IN CONTENTMENT

The way to happiness does not lie in attempting to bring our circumstances up to our minds, but our minds down to our circumstances. Many birds wear a finer coat than the lark, nor is there any that dwells in a lowlier home; yet which of the feathered songsters soars so high, or sings so cheerily, or teaches man so well how to leave the day's cares and labors for the bosom of his family, as when, neither envying the peacock his splendid plumage, nor the proud eagle her lofty realm, it drops singing into its grassy nest to caress its young, and with its wings to shield them from the cold dews of the night? Let ours be the cheerful happiness of Him who, content with little, pleased with whatever pleases the Father, careful for nothing, thankful for anything, prayerful for and in everything, can say with Paul, "I have learned in whatsoever state I am, to be content."—GUTHRIE.

CHEERFULNESS GOOD FOR THE HEALTH

One reason why godliness is profitable unto the things of the life that now is, is because it cultivates cheerfulness, and cheerfulness is good for a man's physical health. It will not restore a broken down constitution, or drive rheumatism from the limbs, or neuralgia from the temples, or pleurisy from the side; but it puts one in such a condition as is most favorable for physical health. That I believe, and that I avow. Everybody knows that buoyancy of spirit is good physical advantage. Gloom, unrest, dejection are at war with every pulsation of the heart, and with every respiration of the lungs. It lowers the vitality, it slackens the circulation, while exhilaration of spirit pours the very balm of heaven through all the currents of life.—TALMAGE.

LIVING IN AN ATMOSPHERE OF CHEERFULNESS

A man's house should be on the hill top of cheerfulness and serenity, so high that no shadows rest upon it, and where the morning comes so early, and the evening tarries so late, that the days has twice as many golden hours as those of other men. He is to be pitied whose house is in some valley of grief between the hills, with the longest night and the shortest day. Home should be center of joy, equatorial and tropical.—BEECHER.

THE CHRISTIAN'S PRIVILEGE

The same Lord who hath bidden us "quit yourselves like men; be strong," has also said, "Rejoice in the Lord alway." The believer's life has its sweets, and these are of the choicest: What is more joyful than the joy of a saint, what more happy than the happiness of a believer? I will not condescend to make a comparison between our joy and the mirth of fools; I will go no further than a contrast. Their mirth is as the crackling of thorns, which spit fire, and make a noise and a flash, but there is no heat, and they are soon gone out, nothing come of it. But the Christian's delight is like a steady coal fire. You have seen the grate full of coals all burning red, and the whole mass of coal has seemed to be one great glowing ruby, and everybody who has come into the room out of the cold has delighted to warm his hands, for it gives out a steady heat. Such are our joys. I would sooner possess the joy of Christ five minutes, than the mirth of fools for half a century.—SPURGEON.

CHEERFULNESS HELPFUL TO OTHERS

God has put us here to make the world brighter, happier and better by our lives, and by helping bear one another's burdens. Every one of us should study how he can be a blessing to others. Let us cheer up the discouraged. If the love of God beats in warm pulsations in our hearts, how easy it will be to win souls for Christ! I have known a whole family to be won to Christ by a smile. We must get the wrinkles out of our brows, and we must have smiling faces. The world is after the best thing, and we must show them that we have something better than they have.—MOODY.

CHILDREN

"But Jesus said suffer little children, and forbid them not, to come unto me, for of such is the kingdom of heaven"—Matt, 19:14.

> "Is anything so innocent,
> So lovely sweet and mild,
> As the budding thought, the untrained soul
> Of a tender little child?"
> —CHARLES B. MANLY.

CHILDREN GONE

Some are from infancy light and happy—they romp, they fly. You can hear their swift feet in the hall. Their loud laughter rings through the house, or in the woods bursts into a score of echoes. At night you can hardly hush their glad hearts for slumber, and in the morning they wake you with their singing. Alas! if then they leave you, and you no more hear their swift feet in the hall, and their loud laughter through the house, or in the woods bursting into a score of echoes; if they wake you no more in the morning with their sweet song; if the color go out of the rose and the leaves fall; if angels for once grow jealous, and want what you cannot spare; if packed away in the trunk or drawer there be silent garments that once. fluttered with youthful life, and by mistake you call some other child by the name of the one departed—ah me! ah me! —TALMAGE.

HOW TO TREAT CHILDREN

There are many persons who have heard so much of family government that they think there cannot be too much of it They imprison their children in stiff rooms, where a fly is a band of music in the empty silence, and govern at morning, at noon, and at night, and the child goes all day long like a shuttle in the loom, back and forward, hit at both sides. Children subjected to such treatment are apt to grow up infidels, through mere disgust.

Many children grow up like plants under bell glasses. They are surrounded only by artificial and prepared influences. There are house-bred, room-bred nurse-bred, mother-bred—everything but self-bred. The object of training is to teach the child to take care of himself; but many parents use their children only as a kind of spool on which to reel off their own experience; and they are bounded and corded until they perish by inanity, or break all bonds and cords, and rush to ruin by reaction.— BEECHER.

PATIENCE WITH CHILDREN

In planting beans the old practice was to put three in each hill: one for the worm, one for the crow, and one to live and produce the crop. In teaching children, we must give line upon line, and precept upon precept, repeating the truth which we would inculcate, till it becomes impossible for the child to forget it. We may well give the lesson once, expecting the child's frail memory to lose it, twice reckoning that the devil, like an ill bird will steal it, thrice, hoping that it will take root downward, and bring forth fruit upward to the glory of God.—SPURGEON.

BRAVE CHILDREN

When the Lawrence mills were on fire a number of years ago, after they had fallen in there was only one room left entire, and in it were three mission Sunday-School children imprisoned. The crowd got shovels, and picks, and crowbars, and were soon working to set the children free, Night came on, and they had not yet reached the children. When they were near them, by some mischance a lantern broke and the ruins caught fire. They tried to put it out but could not succeed. They could talk with the children and even pass them some food, and encourage them to keep up. But, alas, the flames drew nearer and nearer to this prison. Superhuman were the efforts made to rescue the children; the men fought bravely back the flames; but the fire gained fresh strength and returned to claim its victims. The efforts of the fireman were hopeless. When the children knew their fate, they knelt down and commenced to sing the little hymn they had been taught in their Sunday-school days, O, how sweet—: "Let others seek a home below, where flames devour and waves overflow." The flames had now reached them; the stifling smoke began to pour in their little room, and they sank, one by one, upon the floor. A few moments more and the fire circled around them and then their souls were taken into the bosom of God.—MOODY.

PROPER SUBJECTS FOR BAPTISM

Hear the argument of some:"What an oversight on the part of the Lord, in the covenant of circumcision, not to observe that a child eight days old could not understand what it was about! What a waste of piety to baptize an infant of days when it cannot understand what you are doing to it. It cries, poor thing; therefore, how ridiculous to baptize it! It plucks the preacher's gown, or chuckles and coos in the preacher's arms; therefore how absurd to admit it into the covenant I For myself let me say that when I baptize a child I baptise human life,— human life,—life redeemed by the Son of God. The infant is something more than an infant, it is humanity; it is an heir of Christ's immortality. God not only baptizes great trees, but the daisies as well. He enriches Lebanon and Bashan with rain, but does He not also hang the dew of the morning upon the shrinking rose? Account for it as you please, children are under the covenant.

The child does not understand the alphabet, do not teach it You say the child will understand by and by; exactly so; that answer is good; and by and by the child will understand that it was baptised in the name of the Father, and of the Son, and of the Holy Ghost, three persons in one God.—PARKER.

A CHILDREN'S HEAVEN

Heaven is greatly made up of little children—sweet buds that have never blown, or which death has plucked from a mother's bosom to lay on his own cold breast, just when they were expanding flower-like from the sheath, and opening their engaging beauties in the budding time and spring of life. "Of such is the kingdom of heaven." Indeed it may be that God does with his heavenly garden as we do with our own gardens. He may chiefly stock it from nurseries, and select for transplanting what is yet in its young and tender age—flowers before they have bloomed, and trees ere they begin to bear.—GUTHRIE.

CHRIST

"Christ came, who is over all, God blessed forever."—Rom. 9:5.

"Crown Him with many crowns,
 The Lamb upon His throne;
Hark! how the heavenly anthem drowns
 All music but its own.
"Awake, my soul and sing
 Of Him who died for thee,
And hail Him as thy matchless king
 Through all eternity."
 —MATTHEW BRIDGES.

NO NAME LIKE HIS

There is no name like His for us. It is more imperial than Caesar's, more musical than Beethoven's, more conquering than Charlemagne's, more eloquent than Cicero's. It throbs with all life. It weeps with all pathos. It groans with all pain. It stoops with all condescension. It breathes with all perfume. Who like Jesus to set a broken bone, to pity a homeless orphan, to nurse a sick man, to take a prodigal back without any scolding, to illumine a cemetery all ploughed with graves, to make a queen unto God out of the lost woman of the street, to catch the tears of human sorrow in a lachrymatory that never shall be broken? Who has such an eye to see our need, such a lip to kiss away our sorrow, such a hand to snatch us out of the fire, such a foot to trample our enemies, such a heart to embrace all our necessities?—TALMAGE.

HIS COMPASSION

The miracles of Christ were, almost all of them, mere acts of benevolence. He was poor; he had neither raiment nor money to give; and yet there was suffering round about him, and he relieved it. The miracles of Christ were never wrought in an ostentatious way. Never were they wrought for the purpose of exalting himself. They were not employed by Him when arguments failed, to carry men away by superstitious enthusiasm. Multitudes resorted to Him for help—the sick, the blind, the deaf, lepers, all kinds of unfortunate people; and miracles were His means of bestowing charity upon them. No hospital had He to which He could send them; He was His own hospital. His miracles were His general acts of kindness. As laid down in the gospel they represent the heart of God.—BEECHER.

THE GLORIOUS CONQUEROR

Christ has forever overcome all His foes, and divided the spoil upon the battle-field, and now, even at this day, is He enjoying the well-earned reward of His fearful struggle. Lift up your eyes to the battlements of Heaven— the great metropolis of God. The pearly gates are wide open, and the city shines with her jeweled walls like a bride adorned for her husband. Do you see the angels crowding to the battlements? At last there is heard the Song of a trumpet, and the angels hurry to the gates— the army of the redeemed. "The church of the first-born" is approaching the city. Hark to the shout of acclamation! "Behold the Lord cometh with ten thousands of His saints." Hearken to them as they enter. Every one of them waving his helmet in the air, cries, "Unto Him that loved us, and washed us from our sins in His bloody unto Him be honor, and glory, and dominion, and power, for ever and ever."

Mark the heroes as they march along the golden streets, everywhere meeting an enthusiastic welcome from the angels who have kept their first estate. On, on they pour, those countless legions—was there ever such a spectacle? For four thousand years streams on the army of Christ's redeemed. But see! He comes. I see his immediate herald, clad in a garment of camel's hair, and a leathern girdle about His loins. The Prince of the house of David is not far behind. Let every eye be open. He comes! He comes! He comes! It is Christ Himself! Lash the snow-white coursers up the everlasting hills; "Lift up your heads, O, ye gates, and be ye lifted up ye everlasting doors, that the King of Glory may come in." See, He enters in the midst of acclamations. It is He! but He is not crowned with thorns. It is He! but though His hands wear the scar, they are stained with blood no longer. His eyes are as a flame of fire, and on His head are many crowns, and He hath on His vesture and on His thigh written, KING OF KINGS, AND LORD OF LORDS. Clothed in a vesture dipped in blood, He stands confessed the emperor of heaven and earth.—SPURGEON.

WORTHY TO RECEIVE PRAISE

We are told that when John was in the spirit on the Lord's day, and being caught up, he heard a shout around him, ten thousand times ten thousand, and thousands of thousands of voices, "Worthy is the Lamb that was slain to receive power, and riches, and wisdom, and strength, and honor, and glory, and blessing." Yes, He is worthy of all this. Heaven can not speak too well of Him. Oh, that earth would take up the echo, and join with heaven in singing that doxology. I would to

God that I had the voice of an angel, that I might win your soul to the Son of God. A man was preaching in Brooklyn to-day about the white robes, and a friend said the halls of that building never heard such preaching before. And the minister said they might be wearing those robes a good deal sooner than they thought. And just as he got through he drew up both his hands and said, "Jesus," and fell dead. Would that I could stand aside and let him take my place for five minutes.—MOODY.

HIS CROWN

There are crowns worn by living monarchs, of which it would be difficult to estimate the value. The price paid for their jewels is the least part of it. They cost thousands of lives and rivers of human blood; yet in His esteem, and surely in ours also, Christ's crown outweighs them all. He gave his His life for it; and alone, of all monarchs, He was crowned at His coronation by the hands of Death. Others cease to be kings when they die. By dying He became a king. He laid His head in the dust that He might become "head over all," He entered His kingdom through the gates of the grave, and ascended the universe bj the steps of a cross.—GUTHRIE.

THE INTERPRETER OF LIFE

Life is a dream, a riddle, a mystery, a difficult problem. But there is one interpreter. What is his name? Where can he be found? His name is Jesus Christ, and he can be found wherever there is a heart that wants him. You have a dream—you cannot call it by any other name— about sin. You know there is something wrong somewhere. You cannot explain it; you cannot set it down in order, proposition after proposition. It is as unsubstantial as a dream, and impalpable as a vision. Yet it haunts you and you want to know more about it. Christ is the Interpreter, and He alone can explain what sin is; show it in its reality, and give the soul to feel how terrible a thing it is. You have dreams about truth. Sometimes you see an image that you think is the very image of truth herself. Sometimes that angel comes quite near you, and you are almost on the point of laying your hand on the glittering vision. You cannot quite do so. It leaves you, escapes you, mocks you! Jesus Christ is the Interpreter of that dream. Why? Because he is the truth.—PARKER.

CONFESSION

"My Son, give, I pray thee, glory to the Lord God of Israel and make confession unto him."—Josh. 7:19.

"I bring my sins to Thee,
    The Bins I can not count,
That all may cleansed be,
    In Thy once opened Fount;
I bring them Savior, all to Thee;
    The burden is too great for me,"

UNCONSCIOUS SELF-CONFESSION

A company of persons suspected of crime were brought before a judge. Only one of them was guilty, but bow to find out which one, was the question. The judge put his ear against the heart of each one and listened. When he came to the guilty one, he heard in every thump of his heart an acknowledgment of his crime. And so, though all may seem fair in our case, if we could listen at the door of our hearts, every pulsation would confess, Guilty! Guilty!—TALMAGE.

CONFESSION ASSURES PARDON

If I am working beside a man, and I see that he tries to shirk and shift his labor upon me, I am angry with him. But if he says to me, "I am wounded, and cannot work," or, "I am lame," or, "sick," then the thought comes to me at once, "you shall not work; I will help you." And so if a man says to us, "I know I did wrong; but I am weak. Blame me as little as you can," that very confession disarms us, and we think better of him than we did before.

Therefore it is that God so exhorts us to confess our sins to Him. God is like us to this extent that whatever in us is good, is like God.—BEECHER.

COMING TO THE KING AS A BEGGAR

A great monarch was accustomed on certain set occasions to entertain all the beggars of the city. Around him were placed his courtiers, all clothed in rich apparel; the beggars sat at the same table in their rags of poverty. Now it came to pass that on a certain day, one of the courtiers had spoiled his silken apparel, so that he dared not put it on, and he felt, "I can not go to the King's feast to-day, for my robe is foul." He sat weeping till the thought struck him, "To-morrow when the King holds his feast, some will come as courtiers happily decked in their beautiful array, but others will come and be made quite as welcome who will be dressed in rags. Well, well," said he, "so long as I may see the King's face, and sit at the royal table, I will enter among the beggars." So without mourning because he had lost his silken habit, he put on the rags of a beggar and saw the King's face as well as if he had worn the scarlet and fine linen. My soul has done this full many a time, when her evidences of salvation have been dim; and I bid you do the same when you are in like case, if you cannot come to Jesus as a saint, come as a sinner; only do come with simple faith to Him, and you shall receive joy and peace. —SPURGEON.

CONFESSION A CONDITION OF BLESSING

When Job was confessing his sin, God turned his captivity and heard his prayer. God will hear our prayer and turn our captivity when we take our true place before Him, and confess and forsake our transgressions. It was when Isaiah cried out before the Lord, "I am undone," that the blessing came. It was when David said, "I have sinned!" that God dealt in mercy with him. Jonah was cast into the sea, and there was an ease in the ship; Achan was stoned and the plague was stayed. Out with Jonah, out with Achan; and there will follow ease and quiet in the soul presently.—MOODY.

CONFESSION OF PAUL, DAVID AND EZRA

Confession, self-abasement has characterized not prophets and apostles only, but the elect of God in every age of the Church. "I," said St. Paul, "am the chief of sinners." "I," said David, "was as a beast before Thee." "I," said Ezra, "am ashamed, and blush to lift up my face to Thee, O my God;" and so certainly does a man grow humbler as he grows holier. It is with self-esteem as with the column of mercury in the tube of a barometer—the higher we ascend, it sinks the lower. What more striking illustration than that of Heaven itself affords? There, purified from all conceit and pride, perfect both in humility and in holiness, the saints, as if unworthy to wear on their heads wn&t Jesus won on His cross, cast their crowns at His feet.— GUTHRIE.

CONSCIENCE

"And herein do I exercise myself, to have always a conscience void of offense toward God, and toward men."—Acts 24:16.

"What stronger breast-plate than a heart untainted?
Thrice is he armed that hath his quarrel just;
And he but naked though locked up in steel,
Whose conscience with unjustice is corrupted."
—SHAKESPEARE, HENRY VI.

"The mind that broods o'er guilty woes
So like the scorpion girt by fire."
—BYRON.

AN APARTMENT OF THE SOUL

Conscience is an apartment of the soul—an apartment wonderfully constructed. It seems to be central. It is connected with every other apartment in the dwelling. On examination, however, it will be found that, for the most part, the doors are all locked. The floor is thick with dust. The dust is its carpet. The room is very dark. The windows are glazed over with webbed dirt. The light is shut out and the whole apartment is dismal. The man who owns the house does not frequent this room.— BEECHER.

CONSCIENCE MAY BECOME HARDENED

It is a very terrible thing to let conscience begin to grow hard, for it soon chills into northern iron and steel. It is like the freezing of a pond. The first film of ice is scarcely perceptible; keep the water stirring and you will prevent the frost from hardening it; but once let it film over and remain quiet, the glaze thickens over the surface, and it thickens still, and at last is so firm that a wagon might be drawn over the solid ice. So with conscience, it films over gradually, until at last it becomes hard and unfeeling, and is not crushed even with ponderous loads of iniquity.— SPURGEON.

CONSCIENCE UNIVERSALLY SIN-STRICKEN

The universal conscience of mankind is stricken with a sense of guilt Alarmed by an instinctive sense of danger, men have felt the need of reconciliation; and under a sense of His displeasure, have everywhere and in all ages, sought to make their peace with God. For this end altars were raised, and temples were built; sacrifices offered, and penances endured. If the colossal structures of Egypt, and the lovely temples of Greece and Borne, were erected, as well to adorn the state as to please the gods, it was less to please approving, than to appease angry divinities, that their courts resounded with the cries of victims, and smoking altars ran red with blood. So much did the heathen feel their need of peace, such store did they set by it, that many of them sought it at any price. They would buy peace at any cost; nor did they shrink from giving all their fortune, even the fruit of their body, for the sin of their souls. For peace with God, the Hindu walked to his distant temples in sandals that, set with spikes, pierced his flesh at every step, and marked all the long, slow, painful journey with a track of blood; for peace with God, the Syrian led his sweet boy up to the fires of Moloch, and, unmoved in purpose by cries, or curses, or passionate entreaties, cast him shrieking on the burning pile; for peace with God the Indian mother approached the river's brink with streaming eyes and trembling steps, and tearing the suckling from her bursting heart, kissed it, to turn away her eyes, and fling it into the flood.—GUTHRIE.

CONSCIENCE KEEPS A RECORD

Conscience obeyed, or conscience violated, records itself upon the judgment leaf, that one leaf in every human heart. You have known persons who were near drowning, but they were afterwards resuscitated, and they have told you that in the two or three minutes between the accident and the resuscitation, all their past life flashed before them, all they had ever thought, all they had ever done, all they had ever seen in an instant came before them. The memory never loses anything. It is only a folded leaf. It is only a closed book. Though you be an octogenarian, though you be a nonagenarian, all the thoughts and acts of your life are recorded by conscience on memory's page, whether you recall them or not. That leaf, that judgment leaf in my heart, that judgment leaf in your heart, will decide our condition after this world shall have five thousand million years been swept out the heavens, an extinct planet, and time itself will be so long past that on the ocean of eternity it will seem only as now seems a ripple on the Atlantic.— TALMAGE.

CONSOLATION

"As ye are partakers of the sufferings, so shall ye be also of the consolation."—2 Cor. 1:7.

A lily said to a threatening cloud,
    That in sternest garb arrayed him,
"You have taken my Lord, the Sun, away
    And I know not where you have laid him.",

"It folded its leaves, and trembled sore
    As the hours of darkness pressed it,
But at morn, like a bird, in beauty shone,
    For with pearls the dews had dressed it."

"Then it felt ashamed of its fretful thought,
    And fain in the dust would hide it,
For the night of weeping had jewels brought,
    Which the pride of day denied it."
        —MRS. SIGOURNEY.

COMFORT IN VIEW OF REWARD

If you are ever so low now remember that

    "A few more rolling suns, at most,
        Will land thee on fair Canaan's coast."

    Thy head may be crowned with thorny troubles now, but it shall wear a starry crown directly; thy hand may be filled with cares—it shall grasp a harp soon, a harp full of music. Thy garments may be soiled with dust now; they shall be white by and by. Wait a little longer. Ah! beloved, how despicable our trials and troubles will seem when we look back upon them! Look at them here in the prospect, they seem immense; but when we get to Heaven, we shall then,

> "With transporting joys recount
> The labors of our feet."

Our trials will seem to us nothing at all. We shall talk to one another about them in Heaven, and find all the more to converse about, according as we have suffered more here below. Let us go on, therefore; and if the night be ever so dark, remember there is no night without a morning; and that morning is to come by and by.—SPURGEON

WORDS FOR WEEPING MOTHERS

A lady had a little child that was dying. She thought it was resting sweetly in the arms of Jesus. She went into the room and the child asked her: "What are those clouds and mountains that I see so dark?" "Why, Eddy," said his mother, "there are no clouds nor mountains, you must be mistaken." "Why, yes, I see great mountains, and dark clouds, and I want you to take me in your arms and carry me over the mountains." "Oh," said the mother, "you must pray to Jesus, He will carry you safely." My friends the dear mother, the praying mother, may come to your bedside and wipe the damp sweat from your brow, but they cannot carry you over Jordan when the hour comes. This mother said to her little boy, "you must pray that the Lord will be with you in your dying moments." And the two prayed, but the boy turned to her and said: "Don't you hear the angels, mother, over the mountains, calling for me, and I cannot go?" "My dear boy, pray to Jesus, and He will come; He alone can take you." And the boy closed his eyes and prayed, and when he opened them a heavenly smile overspread his face as he said, "Jesus has come to carry me over the mountains." What consolation for the mother, to know her little one was with Jesus.— MOODY.

WEEP NOT AS THOSE THAT HAVE NO HOPE

If a God had died, the terror and grief could barely have exceeded that I once saw in the case of a mother who had set her affections on the child we had met to carry to the grave. Seated at the head of the coffin, she seemed a statue; the grand work of some master hand, to represent the deepest, blackest grief. No tears were on her bloodless cheek. Fixed on the coffin, her eyes never left it. She neither moved nor spake, as on her face one could read these words, "my heart is withered like grass." Absorbed in shadow, it mattered as little to her as to the dead, who went out, or who came in. At length the moment came to remove the body. Then, as when the heavens that have been gathering blackness break out into a blaze of flame and roar of thunder, burst the storm. The form that had looked more like lifeless marble than one animate with life? now sprung up, threw itself on the coffin, clung to it with wails to pierce a heart of stone; and, when gentle force was employed to unloose her arms, she walked to the door patting the poor coffin; and saw it borne out of her sight with an expression of agony, which, as she fell fainting back into the arms of kind neighbors, seemed to cry, "Ye have taken away my god, and what have I more?"

It is not so we are to love our dear ones. We are to love our children as they are to obey their parents, "in the Lord;" never forgetting that He who lends may resume His gifts whensoever it pleases Him, and so ever seeking our nurseries to rear plants for heaven, and so train up our children in the faith, that we shall have the infinite consolation of knowing, if death enters our house and plucks them from our arms, that our loss is their gain; that if a chair in the circle by our fireside is empty, a blood-bought throne is filled in heaven; that if there is one voice less in the psalm when we are assembled for worship, there is one more ringing sweet and clear in glory, praising Him through whose dying love and in blissful presence we shall join our loved—to weep and to part no more. Blessed Hope! Sweet Comfort! Everlasting Consolation!— GUTHRIE.

COMFORT AS OF A MOTHER

"As one whom a mother comforteth, so will I comfort you." You know there is no cradle song like a mother's. After the excitement of the evening it is almost impossible to get the child to sleep. If the rocking-chair stop a moment, the eyes are wide open; but the mother's patience and the mother's soothing manner keep on until, after a while, the angel of slumber puts his wing over the pillow. Well, my dear brothers and sisters in Christ, the time will come when we will be waiting to be put to sleep. The day of our life will be done, and the shadows of the night of death will be gathering round us. Then we want God to soothe us, to hush us to sleep. Let the music at our going not be the dirge of the organ, or the knell of the church-tower, or the drumming of a "dead march," but let it be the consoling hush of a mother's lullaby. Oh, the cradle of the grave will be soft with the pillow of all the promises. When we are being rocked into our last slumber, I want this to be the cradlesong: "As one whom a mother comforteth, so will I comfort you."—TALMAGE.

LIKE SUNSHINE THRO' CLOUD

There are happy and easy souls that are buoyed up by inward hopefulness and outward prosperities, who can hardly understand the need of so much being said about God's consolations, and who scarcely derive any light or comfort from those numerous passages in the word of God that to others are like water in the wilderness. In God's words of promise, comfort and cheer, there is a singular sweetness when they are regarded as voices sent down to men in their struggles through life. They are like open glades in a dark forest, where the sun lies on warm banks, the father of many flowers. And so these openings with summer in them have peculiar relish and charm to many. —BEECHER.

CONVERSION

"Repent ye therefore, and be converted."—Acts 3:19.

"Oh, happy day! When first I felt
My soul with deep contrition melt,
And saw my sins of crimson guilt,
All cleansed by blood on Calvary spilt."

RESTITUTION

When Zaccheus was converted, he gave half his goods to the poor. He did more than that; he said, "if I have taken anything from any man, falsely, I will restore him fourfold." It made a great stir in Jericho. The people said, "there is a true disciple." His conversion was like a flashing meteor—so sudden. You must remember one thing—conversion means something. If you don't give half your goods to feed the poor, you must make restitution. If you have lied about a man, if you have slandered a man, if you have abused a man, go and tell him you have done him an injustice; go and make restitution. I felt much encouraged last night; a man came into the inquiry room and said, "Mr. Moody, I want you to forgive me." "Why," said I, "I have got nothing to forgive you for; I never met you before." "Well," said the man, "I have been abusing you for about a year. I was here last night, and I got converted, and I want your forgiveness." There was a man in Brooklyn who, after his conversion, said; "There is a shoemaker's bill I've been owing for nine years; I'll go and pay it." He did so, and the shoemaker said, "Well, I believe in that kind of meetings now." He didn't believe in them before. Conversion implies discipleship to Jesus Christ.—MOODY.

DATE OF CONVERSION

Some can tell the time of their conversion, giving day and date, the hour, the providence, the place, the text, the preacher, and all the circumstances associated with it. They can show the arrow, which, shot from some bow drawn at a venture, pierced the joints of their armor, and quivered in their heart. They can show the pebble from the brook, that, slung, it may be, by a youthful hand, but directed of God, was buried in the forehead of their giant sin. It is not so however with all, or perhaps with most. Some, so to speak, are still born; they were unconscious of their change; they did not know when or how it happened; for a while at least they gave hardly a sign of life.— GUTHRIE.

REVIVAL CONVERSIONS

I have more faith (put this down in your memorandum-book), I have more faith in men who are brought to God during revivals than during a frigid state of the church. I have had close observation in these things. Stand two men side by side. Let them have equal endowments. You tell me that this man was brought in when the church was very cold, and the other was brought in while the church was very warm in revivals. I will say, "Give me the last one; I had rather have him than five of the other kind.

When are we going to get the world converted? When the people in solid columns march into the Kingdom of God, not by ones, but by tens, fifties and hundreds,. Oh, that the Lord would upturn this church with holy revivals! Oh, that such days might come as Richard Baxter saw in Kidderminster, as Jonathan Edwards saw in Northampton, as McCheyne saw in Dundee! "O, Lord, revive thy work!"—TALMAGE.

FEELING NOT AN INDEX OF CONVERSION

There are many persons whose conversion is a long and severe struggle, during which they alternate week after week, and month after month between hope and fear, who, were it not for perplexing their minds with a wrong notion of what they are to do and be done with, might go up the mountain almost without going through the valley. It is known that John Wesley went well nigh three years before he found what he sought. John Bunyan went through awful terrors, as a consequence of a long continued exercise of mind, before he found religious peace. His experiences are embalmed in some of the best writing in the English language. It is my impression that the conversion of Bunyan might as well have been a work of days as of months. The difficulty in many cases results from an erroneous apprehension of what is to be taken as evidence of conversion, Now, to be a Christian is to obey Christ, no matter how you feel. If a person trying to come into the discipleship of Christ, expects to do so by sitting down and waiting for a certain preconceived state of mind to come to him, as he might wait for a pair of wings to sprout out of his shoulders, he must not be surprised if he is disappointed.—BEECHER.

CONVERSION A SIMPLE DOCTRINE

When we preach fine sermons our hearers say, "That was prettily put." They do not so much notice what we taught, as how we taught it, and this is a great evil. Even so if you go and talk about your salvation to your neighbor, and narrate it eloquently, she will say, "Mrs. So-and-so has been here, and told me about her conversion in such beautiful language; I do not know that I ever heard such elegant sentences; it was most delightful to hear her." "What did she say?" "I do not know what she said, but it was very beautiful." Thus many a sermon is overlaid and buried under its own robes. Conversion is a simple doctrine. Pity that those we seek to bless should be more taken up with our pretty words than with the truth of our adorable master.—SPURGEON.

COURAGE

"He thanked God and took courage."—Acts 28:15.

>Dare to be a Daniel,
>Dare to stand alone,
>Dare to have a purpose true,
>Dare to make it known.

THE CHRISTIAN A SOLDIER

To watch, to fight, with steady front to meet and repel temptation—in other words to do no evil, is, however, though an important part, but one, and not the most important part of Christian work. The Church of the Living God bears no resemblance to those communities of ants where a certain number of these curious insects form a sort of standing army, and have no other duties but to defend and battle for the commonwealth; the building, and provisioning, and other duties of the ant hill belonging to the others, and not to them, nor to take an illustration from the arrangements of human society, does Christ's kingdom resemble this, or that of any other sovereign, where the military, wearing a distinct garb, and exempted from those productive labors whereby others support themselves, and add to the wealth of the country, form a distinct order of the community. The type of a Christian is seen not in lands where citizens and soldiers, working and fighting men from different classes; but rather in those troubled regions of the East, where the husbandman, constantly exposed to the attack of murderers and robbers, ploughs the soil with a carbine slung at his back, or a sword slung at his side. The true Christian must be a soldier, and he must be a true soldier, bold, courageous and active in defensive and aggressive warfare.—GUTHRIE

GRACE FOR COURAGE

The father does not give to his son at school enough money to last him several years, but as the bills for tuition and board and clothing and books come in, pays them, so God will not give you grace all at once for the future, but will meet all your exigencies as they come. Then courage, my brother, courage!—TALMAGE.

COURAGE ON BEHALF OF PRINCIPLE

Do not be afraid to spend yourself. Do not hesitate to risk yourself. Do not shrink from treading on principle. It will carry you, as a bridge, over the deepest and darkest chasm that exists. Trust truth, and purity, and integrity, and benevolence. Give yourself to them. Throw yourself impetuously, enthusiastically, into them. And do not wait to see if anybody sees you. Do not care what anybody says. Be unconscious so far as men are concerned. Be boldly true and truly bold.—BEECHER

MEMORY AN AID TO COURAGE

Sir Francis Drake being in a dangerous storm in the Thames, was heard to say, "Must I who have escaped the rage of the ocean, be drowned in a ditch?" Will you, experienced saints, who have passed through a world of tribulation, lie down and die of despair, or give up your profession because you are at the present moment passing through some light affliction? Let your past preservation inspire you with courage, and constrain you to brave all storms for Jesus' sake. Courage for the present is strengthened by the memory of past deliverances.—SPURGEON.

GOD USES BOLD MEN

See Elijah on Mount Carmel, full of boldness. How the Lord used him! How the Lord stood by him! How the Lord blessed him! But when he got his eyes off the way, and Jezebel sent a message to him that she would have his life, he got afraid. He was not afraid of Ahab and the whole royalty, not afraid of all the nation. He stood on Mount Carmel alone, and see what courage he had! But what came over him, I don't know, unless it was that he got his eyes off the Lord. That, I think, is the trouble with a good many of God's people. We get frightened, and are afraid to speak to men about their souls. We lack moral courage. The work of soul-saving will not begin until we get the courage to invite men to Christ, personally. We read that when the Apostles were brought before the council, they perceived their boldness, and it made an impression on the council. The Lord could use them then because they were fearless and bold.—MOODY.

RIGHT AGAINST MIGHT

Will you do nothing to put down the evil side of that foolish proverb, "Nothing succeeds like success?" Beard success in its own den, fight the most popular evils, espouse the poorest and the weakest causes, if you believe that they are inspired by one element of right. It takes a strong man to stand alone. It is only a man here and there that can raise a tune; almost everybody tries to have a mumble after it is raised. But stand alone, young friend; stand alone, poor man; stand with the right. We are in the minority, but we are in the minority of God. I do not believe in majorities, popularly so called. I believe men should be weighed as well as numbered. I would rather have the support of one man of a certain kind, than the support of ten thousand of a kind directly opposite. —PARKER.

CREATION

"In the beginning God created the heaven and the earth."— Gen. 1:1.

"Load hallelujahs to the Lord,
    From distant worlds, where creatures dwell;
Let heaven begin the solemn word,
    And sound it dreadful down to hell.
Wide as his vast dominion lies,
    Make the Creator's name be known;
Loud as his thunder shout his praise,
    And sound it lofty as his throne."

CREATION IN A CIRCLE

God created the universe on the plan of a circle. There are in the natural world straight lines, angles, parallelograms, diagonals, quadrangles; but these evidently are not God's favorites. Giant's Causeway in Ireland shows what God thinks of mathematics. There are over thirty-five thousand columns of rocks—octagonal, hexagonal, pentagonal. These rocks seem to have been made by rule and compass. Every artist has his moulding room, where he may make fifty shapes; but he chooses one shape as preferable to all the others. I will not say that the Giant's Causeway was the world's moulding room, but I do say, out of a great many figures, God seems to have selected the circle as the best. He created the stars in a circle, the universe in a circle, and the throne on which He sits is the center of that circle.—TALMAGE.

CULTURE THE COMPLEMENT OF CREATION

Creation begins the work. Culture continues it. There is but a beginning in natural fruits, and they never, when left to nature alone, reach beyond that point. When a man finds a crab apple in the woods, he would not willingly find it more than once; yet, brought to his own orchard, it becomes a fine fruit. But did nature make the pippin? Nature had been trying her hand for years and years, and had never been able to get beyond the crab apple. Man says to her: "You are a bungling apprentice; I will make you a journeyman." Iron is created, but a sword is made. Nature does not create a jack-knife, a steam engine, a knife and fork, but bare, cold, dead iron. God intends that we shall only do the work of utilizing, He of creating, for that we can not do.—BEECHER.

GOD IN CREATION

Phidias, the Grecian sculptor, needed not to have the name Phidias in so many letters on his work, for the master's hand had a cunning of its own which none could counterfeit. An instructed person had only to look at the statue and say at once, "Phidias did this, for no other hand could have chiseled such a countenance;" and believers have only to look either at creation, providence, or the divine word, and they will cry instinctively, "This is the finger of God." There is God engraven upon every work of creation.—SPURGEON.

SKILL IN NATURE

The British museum possesses in the Portland vase one of the finest remains of ancient art; and it may be remembered how, some years ago—the world of taste was shocked to hear that this precious relic had been shattered by a maniac's hand. Without disparaging classic taste or this exquisite example of it, I venture to say there is not a poor worm that we tread upon, nor a sere leaf, that, like a ruined but reckless man, dances merrily in its fallen state to the autumn winds, but has superior claims upon our study and admiration. The child who plucks a lily or rose to pieces, or crushes the fragile form of a fluttering insect, destroys a work which the highest art could not invent, nor man's best-skilled hand construct. And there was not a leaf quivered on the trees which stood under the domes of the crystal palace, but eclipsed the brightest glories of loom or chisel; it had no rival among the triumphs of invention, which a world went there to see. In his humblest works, God infinitely surpasses the highest efforts of human skill.—GUTHRIE.

THE CROSS

"God forbid that I should glory save in the cross of our Lod Jesus Christ."—Gal. 6:14.

In the cross of Christ I glory,
   Towering o'er the wrecks of time;
All the light of sacred story
   Gathers round its head Sublime."
        —SIR JOHN BOWRING.

CHRIST WITH US MEANS THE CROSS FOR US

When God breaks up your plans, and throws you to the very ground, and breaks all the threads in the loom which you were weaving, and says to you, "Begin again," is there any Christ for you at that point of your overthrow? Can you go forth unto your Savior marking that place in His life where He was overthrown, identifying it in some way with your own overthrow? Can you stand rejoicing with Christ at that very point of humiliation and crucifixion? Christ may be followed in two ways—victorious, and in disgrace and ignominy; and we are called to follow, first, not Christ as He is set forth in all the royalty of philosophy and reason, but a Christ humiliated, a Christ despised; a Christ hated, a Christ crucified. Before we stand with Christ upon Olivet, we must stand with Him upon Calvary, must walk with Him thither.—BEECHER.

SPES UNICA

On a huge cross by the side of an Italian highway hung a hideous caricature of the Beloved of our souls, who poured out His life for our redemption. Out of reverence to the living Savior we turned aside, disgusted from the revolting image, but not until we had espied the words, "Spes Unica" in capitals over its head. Here was truth emblazoned on an idol. Yes, indeed, Jesus our once crucified, but now exalted Lord, is the sole and only hope of man. The cross bears the Spes Unica to our soul.—SPURGEON.

JESUS BORE THE CROSS FOR US

You ladies wear small crosses made of gold and wood and stone about your necks; but the cross that the Son of God carried was a rude, heavy tree, made into a cross. I can imagine Him reeling and staggering under it. Undoubtedly He had lost so much blood that He was too faint to carry it, and before they got to the place, it well nigh crushed Him to the earth. And then some stranger undertook to bear it along after Him. That was only nine o'clock in the morning. They arrived at Calvary a little before nine. Then they took up the Son of God and they laid Him out upon that cross. I can imagine them binding His wrists to the arms of the cross. And after they got Him bound, up came a soldier with a hammer and nails and put one nail into the palm of His hand, and then came the hammer without mercy, driving it down through the bone and flesh and into the wood; and then into the other hand. And then they brought a long nail for His feet. O, you young ladies, who say you see no beauty in Christ that you should desire to be like Him, come with me and take a look at those wounds, and remember that that crown of thorns was laid upon His brow by a mocking world. But while they were crucifying Him, He was praying for them. Was there ever such love as that?—MOODY.

OUR SALVATION WROUGHT UPON THE CROSS

Are you trusting in a righteousness of your own! Leave that loom. Are the gossamer threads of your own TOWS and promises ever snapping in your hand, and breaking at every show of the shuttle? The robe of righteousness, a raiment meet for thy soul, and approved of by God, was never woven there. It was wrought upon the cross; and, of color more enduring than Tyrian purple, it is dyed red in the blood of Calvary.—GUTHRIE.

THE THREE CROSSES

The cross! Poets have sung its praise, and sculptors have attempted to commemorate it in marble, and martyrs have clung to it in fire, and Christians dying quietly in their beds have leaned their heads against it. May all our souls embrace it with an ecstacy of affection. Lay hold of that cross, O dying sinner. Everything else will fail you. Without a strong grip of that you perish. Put your hand on that and you are safe, though the world swing from beneath your feet. Oh I that I might engrave on your souls ineffaceably the three crosses, and that if in your waking moments you will not heed, then that in your dream to-night you might see on the hill back of Jerusalem the three spectacles—the right-hand cross showing unbelief, and dying without Christ—the left-hand showing what it is to be pardoned—while the central cross pours upon your soul the sunburst of Heaven as it says: "By all these wounds I plead for thy heart. I have loved thee with an everlasting love. Rivers cannot quench it The floods cannot drown it!"—TALMAGE.

THE CURE FOR TROUBLE

What is the cure for all this social chaos, domestic trouble, secret pain, this wrong-doing as between kings and subjects, fathers and children, man and man? The one cure is the cross of Christ. Have I not preached that with some consistency ever since you knew me? Have I ever given a second prescription for this malady of the world? If I have, oh! allow me now to tear it up, publicly to tear it up, so that nobody can ever patch it together so as to make one word of it through all time. The prescription I will give is given to me. The prescription by which I would abide according to the exhortation of Scripture, the prescription which I would preach to all mankind is this: "The blood of Jesus Christ, God the Son, cleanseth from all sin."—PARKER.

CROSS-BEARING

"If any man will come after me, let him deny himself and take up his cross, and follow me."—Matt. 16:24.

"Only a little while
  Of walking with weary feet,
Patiently oyer the thorny way
  That leads to the golden street."

"Suffer if God shall will,
  And work for him while we may,
From Calvary's cross to Zion's crown,
  Is only a little way."

A HEAVY CROSS

"Jesus, I my cross have taken," was not written in an easy chair, or on a damask curtain. It was written by a young woman, who for Christ's sake had been driven from her father's home; and you account for the pathos of that hymn when I tell you that she dipped the pen in the blood of her own broken heart, and in her tears, wrote—

"Jesus, I my cross have taken
  All to leave and follow Thee:
Naked, poor, despised, forsaken,
  Thou from hence my all shall be."

BATTLE SCARS FOR CHRIST

Oh Christian man, Oh Christian woman! Have you any scars to show in this conflict? When a war is over the heroes have scars to show. One hero rolls back a sleeve and shows a gun-shot fracture, or he pulls down his collar and shows where he was wounded in the neck. Another man says, "I have never had the use of my limb since I was wounded in that great battle." When the last day comes, will we have any wounds to show for Christ! Will we show marks where we have borne the cross?—TALMAGE.

To the end of life the way of Christ is a way of cross-bearing and of self-denial. To the end of life men stand where these two great influences, one from heaven and the other from the bottom of the earth, meet, and whirl all things round about in struggles; and there is where men strive to overcome the old man that is lowest—the appetites; and to endow themselves with the new man—Christ Jesus. Are you willing to stand at that point and identify yourself with all the humiliation and self-sacrifice which are necessary to put down the old man and to endow yourself with the new man that is in Christ Jesus?—BEECHER.

CHRIST OUR EXAMPLE IN CROSS-BEARING

Christ is our great example in cross-bearing. He had not where to lay his head in life, nor a rag to cover him in death, nor anything but a borrowed grave in burial. What manner of persons ought we to be in all unselfishness when we have such a Lord! He hath not said to us in matters of self-denial, "Take up thy cross and go," but "Come, take up thy cross and follow me." Well may the soldiers endure hardness when the king himself roughs it among us; and suffers more than the meanest private in our ranks. My soul, I charge thee, bear thy cross, and look not for ease where Jesus found his death. —SPURGEON.

SMALL CROSSES

Some shrink from bearing their crosses because of their insignificance as well as on account of their heaviness, in other cases. I remember hearing of a person who was always trying to do some great thing for the Lord, and because he could not do a great thing, he never did anything. There are a great many who would be willing to do great things if they could come up and have their names heralded through the press. Your cross may be an humble one. Don't slight it.—MOODY.

AFTER THE CROSS THE CROWN

Now for the work, hereafter for the wages; earth for the cross, heaven for the crown. Go thy way, assured that there is not a prayer you utter, nor a word you speak, nor a foot you walk, nor a tear you shed, nor a hand you hold out to the perishing, nor a warning you give to the careless, nor a wretched child you pluck from the streets, nor a visit paid to the widow or fatherless, nor a loaf of bread you lay on a poor man's table, that there is no cross you bear for the sake of God and men, but is faithfully registered in the chronicles of the kingdom, and shall be publicly read that day when Jesus, calling you up perhaps from a post as mean as Mordecai's, shall crown your brows before an assembled world, saying, "Thus it shall be done to the man whom the king delighteth to honor."—GUTHRIE.

DEATH

"The small and great are there; and the servant is free from his master."—Job 3:19.

"Leaves have their time to fall,
And flowers to wither at the North-wind's breath,
And stars to set,—but all,
Thou hast all seasons for thine own, O Death!"
—MRS. HEMANS.

A CHILD'S DEATH

There was a child born in your house. All your friends congratulated you. The other children of the family and of the neighborhood stood amazed looking at the new-comer, and asked a great many questions, genealogical and chronological. You said—and you said truthfully—that a white angel flew through the room and left the little one there. That little one stood with its two feet in the very center of your sanctuary of affection, and with its two hands it took hold of the altar of your soul. But one day there came one of the three scourges of children—scarlet fever, or croup, or diphtheria—and all that bright scene vanished. The great Friend of children stooped down and leaned toward that cradle and took the little one in His arms, and walked away with it into the bower of eternal summer. Death came into your household, but are you not more pure and tender-hearted than you used to be, do you not more patiently waiting for the daybreak, on account of that heavenly visitor?—TALMAGE.

DEATH AND MIGRATION

As birds in the hour of transmigration feel the impulse of southern lands, and gladly spread their wings for the realm of light and bloom, so may we, in the death hour feel the sweet solicitations of the life beyond, and joyfully soar from the chill and shadow of earth to fold our wings and sing in the summer of an eternal Heaven.—BEECHER.

DEATH AND UNMASKING

To-day the world is like a masquerade. High carnival is being held, and men wear their masques and dominoes, and strut about, and we think that man a king, and this a mighty prince, and this a haughty chief. But the time is over for the masque; daylight dawns; strip off your garnishings; every one of you put on your ordinary garments. Who goes out to the unrobing room with greatest confidence? Why, the man who feels that his next dress will be a far more glorious vestment. If any reader of this page seems to be what he is not, let him be wise enough to think of the spade, the shroud, and the silent dust. Let every one among us now put his soul into the crucible, and as we shall test ourselves in the silence of the dying hour, so let us judge ourselves now.—SPURGEON.

DEATH ROBBED OF HIS TERROR

A certain gentleman was a member of the Presbyterian Church. His little boy was sick. When he went home, his wife was weeping, and she said, "Our boy is dying; he has had a change for the worse. I wish you would go in and see him." The father went into the room and placed his hand upon the brow of the dying boy, and the cold, damp sweat was gathering there: the icy hand of death was feeling for the chords of life. "Do you know, my boy, that you are dying?" asked the father. "Am I? Is this death? Do you really think I am dying?" "Yes, my son, your end on earth is near." "And will I be with Jesus tonight?" "Yes, you will be with the Savior." "Father, don't you weep, for when I get there, I will go straight to Jesus and tell Him that you have been trying all your life to lead me to Him." So death was robbed of half his terror, by those words of the Christian child.—MOODY.

COMFORT IN DESOLATE HOMES

Our children may not abide; the earth sounds hollow to the foot—it is so full of graves. Ah! how few gardens are there where death has not left his footprints, when he came to steal away some of our sweetest flowers. Few are the trees standing on this earth, from which he has not lopped off some goodly boughs. In this world, have I not seen one and another stand bleak and branchless; and oh how blessed for the father who has laid the last survivor in the dust, and returns from that saddest funeral to find God waiting for him in his desolate home.—GUTHRIE.

AFTER DEATH,—WHAT?

Like a pendulum I swing from prayer to blasphemy, and back again to prayer; and if I would die at prayer I might go to Heaven, but if I should die at blasphemy I might go to hell, and blaspheme there through the ages, and grow worse, and still worse, until God Himself cannot know me as the child baptized in His own name, and held up in public prayer in the old village church a million years before. I fight, and win, and die. I plant the green vineyard and gather purple grapes, and as the wine foams in the full flagon, I fall down and cannot taste the inviting cheer. I build a high house with roof that wind cannot stir nor storm blow through, and when the blazing fire roars from the gleaming hearth, and Comfort, rosy-faced, beams upon me from the pictured walls, I'm sent for and thrust into the grave and prayed over as a failure hero,—perhaps a failure there; handed over to the resurrection, to the Great Unknown, to Ghostland, and a cold stone with lies on it keeps me well down in the earth.

Jesus save me! Christ redeem me! Lord keep me! God help me!—PARKER.

DECISION

"As for me."—Joshua 24:15.

"Delay not, delay not; the hour is at hand;
The earth shall dissolve and the heaven's shall fade;
The dead, small and great, in the judgment shall stand
What helper, then, brother, shall lend thee his aid?"

BE DECISIVE

How many there are who roll through life performing no higher functions than the swine at the trough! They exercise not their God-given power of will to restrain, to decide, to determine. Round and fat they are; sleek and comely they are; good eaters they are; good drinkers they are; good sleepers they are; and good diers they are—for when they are dead they are out of the way. They are born with a cry; then they eat and drink and sleep; then they die with a wheeze—that is all. And how much are they worth? What are they good for? They are fine as the world goes. Yet my asparagus-bed brings forth as good men as they are. I would as lief have fat vegetables as these men of no firmness, of no decision of character, these men of shambles.—BEECHER.

EXAMPLE OF DECISION

After the defeat of the Romans at the battle of Allia, Rome was sacked, and it seemed as if, at any moment, the Gauls might take the capitol. Among the garrison was a young man of the Fabian family, and on a certain day, the anniversary of a sacrifice returned, when his family had always offered sacrifice upon the Quirinal Hill. This hill was in the possession of the Gauls; but when the morning dawned, the young man took the sacred utensils of his god, went down from the capitol, passed through the Gallic sentries, through the main body, up the hill, offered sacrifice, and came back unharmed. It was always told as a wonder among Roman legends. This is just how the Christian should act when decision for Christ is called for. Though he be a solitary man in the midst of a thousand opponents, let him, at the precise moment when duty calls, fearless of danger, go straight to the appointed spot, do his duty, and remember that consequences belong to God, and not to us. I pray God that after this style we may display decision for Christ.—SPURGEON.

IMMEDIATE DECISION

I urge upon you the need of present decision for the right. Don't delay the answer to this great question, "What shall I do with Jesus?" Accept him now. When you are sick is no time to receive Jesus. When death comes, he often steals in unawares. Some men don't know that death is coming until they are hurried away into the other world without any preparation. How much do you suppose some lost one would give for the opportunity of another decision? How much do you think Agrippa would give to be in Paul's place now? How much do you think those men who heard Christ preach, would give if they had the opportunity you have here this afternoon? I believe that Caiaphas would be very glad to exchange places with John; but it is too late now. All the opportunities are gone.—MOODY.

IMPORTANCE OF DECISION

On decision of character, man's best and eternal interest depends. Our position nearly corresponds to that of Israel on Carmel, when Elijah, standing by the mountain altar, addressed the people, saying, "How long halt ye between two opinions: if the Lord be God, follow Him; but if Baal, then follow him!" Christ with a cross, but heaven behind Him; and Satan with the world glittering in his hand, but hell flaming at his back, stand before us, rival candidates. Each solicits our hands and our heart We must decide between them; the one or the other we must serve. In the vain hope of making much of both worlds, unwilling to perish, but yet unwilling to part from sin, many postpone their decision, and attempt to compromise the matter by offering these rivals a divided allegiance. Futile and vain attempt!—GUTHRIE.

AN EARNEST EXHORTATION

I beg of you, make up your decision this morning to start for the kingdom. "Yes," you say, "I will start, but not now." William III made proclamation, when there was a revolution in the north of Scotland, that all who came and took the oath of allegiance by the 31st of December should be pardoned. MacIan, a chieftain of a prominent clan, resolved to return with the rest of the rebels, but had some pride in being the very last one who should take the oath. He postponed starting for this purpose until two days before the expiration of the term. A snowstorm impeded his way, and before he got up to take the oath and receive a pardon from the throne the time was up and past. While the others were set free, MacIan was miserably put to death. He started too late and arrived too late. In postponing your decision, in like manner, some of you are in prospect of losing forever the amnesty of the Gospel.—TALMAGE.

DIVINITY OF CHRIST

"And they shall call his name Emmanuel, which, being interpreted is, God with us"—Matt.1:23.

>Jesus is God! the solid earth,
>   The ocean broad and bright,
>The countless stars like golden dost,
>   That strew the skies at night,
>The wheeling storm, the dreadful fire,
>   The pleasant, wholesome air,
>The summer's sun, the winter's frost,
>   His own creations were.
>   —P. W. FABER.

CHRIST ALL AND IN ALL

As, with the genius that aspires to immortality, and anticipates the admiration of future ages, the painter leaves his name on a corner of the canvas, so Inspiration, dipping her pen in indelible truth, has inscribed the name of Jesus upon all we see—on sun and stars, flower and tree, rock and mountain, the unstable waters and the firm land; and also on what we do not see, nor shall till death has removed the veil, angels and spirits, the city and heavens of the eternal world. This is no matter of fancy. It is a fact. It is a blessed fact No voice ever sounded more distinctly to my ear, than that of revealed truth, proclaiming Jesus, Lord of all.—GUTHRIE.

HE WAS DIVINE

Christ's work was that of a God. I hear it in his voice; I see it in the flash of his eye; I behold it in the snapping of death's shackles; I see it in the face of the rising slumberers; I hear it in the outcry of all those who were spectators of the scenes. He cleft the sea. He upheaved the crystalline walls along which the Israelites marched. He planted the mountains. He raised up governments, and cast down thrones. He marches across nations, and across worlds, and across the universe, eternal, omnipotent, unhindered, and unabashed. That hand that was nailed to the cross holds the stars in a leash of love. That head that dropped on the bosom in fainting and death shall make the world quake at its nod. That voice that groaned in the last pang shall swear before the trembling world that time shall be no longer. He was a God—a God!—TALMAGE.

HIS DIVINITY MANIFEST IN HIS LOVE

The nature of Divinity as disclosed by Jesus Christ, is uplifting love in a God who does not sit like some old Jupiter seeking his own happiness, and indulging in self-worship; in a God that does not bargain or traffic; in a God of disinterested goodness, who is constantly pouring out his life in suffering, in burden-bearing, for the sake of saving men, and raising them from degradation and misery to a life of happiness and exaltation; in One who walks in sublime purity among men, and comes to his passion knowing what is before him, and drinks the cup to the very dregs, and will not turn back; in One, who for love's sake dies heroically, ascends to heaven, and comes back and bears witness to mankind that they are ascending to His Father and their Father, and says, "Now go and preach to all that tho love of God was made plain to men by the sufferings of his only begotten son, that every man who hears it may know that though he be weak, imperfect and sinful, he has a Friend in heaven."— BEECHER.

THE EXALTED ONE

Look at him, can your imagination picture him? Behold his transcendent glory! The majesty of kings is swallowed up; the pomp of empires dissolves like the white mist of the morning before the sun; the brightness of assembled armies is eclipsed. He, in himself is brighter than the sun, fairer than the moon, more terrible than an army with banners. See him! See him! O! hide your heads, ye monarchs; put away your gaudy pageantry, ye lords of this poor narrow earth! His kingdom knows no bounds; without a limit his vast empire stretches out itself. Above him all is his; beneath him many a step are angels, and they are his; and they cast their crowns before his feet.

With them stand his elect and ransomed, and their crowns too are his. And here upon this lower earth stand his saints, and they are his, and they adore him; and under the earth, among the infernals, where devils growl their malice, even there is trembling and adoration; and where lost spirits, with wailing and gnashing of teeth, forever lament their being, even there is the acknowledgment of his Godhead, even though the confession helps to make the fire of their torment. In heaven, in earth, in hell, all knees bend before him, and every tongue confesses that he is God. If not now, yet in the time that is to come, this shall be carried out, that every creature of God's making shall acknowledge his Son to be "God over all blessed forever. Amen."—SPURGEON.

CHRIST ON TRIAL

When Jesus was on trial, they did not go and summon his friends—those who knew him best They did not go and bring up Zaccheus of Jericho, they did not bring up that poor man that had the legion of devils cast out of him; they did not bring the blind man of Jericho—they brought his enemies. Let Caiaphas tell his own story— suppose he stood in my place. Caiaphas, just tell us what was the evidence you found against Jesus. "I said to him I adjure thee by the living God, art thou the Son of God! And he said 'I am.' When I heard it I tore my mantle and said he was guilty of blasphemy." That is what we glory in, his being the Son of God. Stephen said, when the curtains were lifted, and he caught a glimpse of glory, I see Jesus standing at the right hand of God." The testimony is perfectly overwhelming that Jesus Christ was the Son of God as well as the Son of David. Even the devils called him "that son of the Most High God."— MOODY.

DUTY

"We have done that which was our duty to do."—Luke 17:10.

"Better than ringing plaudits of a throng,
Than voice of multitudes in shouts of praise,
Than smiles of beauty and of rarest grace,
Are silent whispers of a conscience free
From sense of duty left undone."
- CHARLES MANLY.

DUTY VERSUS LOVE

I am tired of the word duty; tired of hearing duty, duty, duty. Men go to church because it is their duty. You can never reach a man's heart if you talk to him because it is your duty. Suppose I told my wife I love her because it is my duty—what would she say? Once every year I go up to Connecticut to visit my aged mother. Suppose when I go next time, I tell her I know she is old and living on borrowed time; that I knew she had done a great deal for me, and that I came to see her every year because it is my duty. Don't you think she would say, "Well, then, my son, you needn't take the trouble to come again?" Oh, let us strike for a higher plane than duty. —MOODY.

EXAMPLE OF LOVE AS COMPARED WITH DUTY

During a heavy storm off the Coast of Spain, a dismasted merchantman was observed by a British frigate drifting before the gale. Every eye and glass were on her. With all his faults, no man is more alive to humanity than the rough and hardy mariner; and so the order sounds to put the ship about, and presently a boat is sent out to bear down upon the wreck. Through the swell of a roaring sea, they reach it; they shout; and now a strange object rolls out of a canvas screen against the lee shroud of a broken mast. Hauled into the boat, it proves to be the trunk of a man, bent head and knees together, so dried and shriveled as to be hardly felt within the ample clothes, and so light that a mere boy lifted it on board. It is laid on the deck; in horror and pity the crew gather round it; it shows signs of life; they draw nearer, it moves, and then mutters—mutters in a deep, sepulchral voice—"There is another man" Saved himself, the first use the saved one made of speech was to save another. Oh! learn that precious lesson. Be daily practicing it. So long as in our homes, among our friends, in this wreck of a world which is drifting down to ruin, there lives an unconverted one, there is "(mother man" let us for God's sake, and for duty's, go to him and plead for Christ; go to Christ and plead for that man; the cry, "Lord save me, I perish," changed into one as welcome to a Savior's ear, "Lord save them, they perish."—GUTHRIE.

COMMONPLACE DUTY

There is no better place from which to see heaven than a carpenter's bench, or a mason's wall, or a merchant's counter, if the heart be right. Elisha was plowing in the field when the prophetic mantle fell upon him. Matthew was engaged in his custom-house duties when he was commanded to "follow." James and John were busily engaged in mending their nets when called to become fishers of men. Had they been snoring in the sun, Christ would not have brought their indolence into the apostleship. Gideon was at work with a flail on a threshing floor when he saw the angel. It was when Saul was with fatigue hunting his father's asses that he got the crown of Israel. There is no post like the post of duty.—TALMAGE

DUTY THIS PENDULUM OF A CLOCK

If you wind up the weights of a clock, and point the hands to the proper figures, and go away, you will find them in the same place when you go away an hour later. Set it again, and an hour later it will be as you left it. What does it need? It needs to have the pendulum swing and then it will keep time. Now, I am continually setting Christians; and when I look again, I find them just as I left them. What all such need is to swing the pendulum of duty. Your hearts must be always ticking, if you would keep time with the Sun of Righteousness.—BEECHER.

THE CHRISTIAN'S DUTY

Oh, Christians, never be satisfied with being merely saved. Up with you! Away off! Go onward, up the path of loving duty to the high mountains, to the clearer light, to the brighter joy. If saved and brought like the shipwrecked mariner to shore, is that enough? Yes, for the moment it is enough to warrant the purest satisfaction and the warmest congratulations. Must the mariner not seek a livelihood as long as he lives? Must he not put forth his energies? Just so let it be with you. Saved from the deep which threatened to swallow you up, rejoice that you are preserved from deathr but resolve that the life vouchsafed to you shall be active, earnest, fruitful, vigorous and dutiful. Be active as your merchants are.—SPURGEON.

EARNESTNESS

"Therefore we ought to give the more earnest heed to the things which we have heard"—Heb. 2:1.

"The busy world shoves angrily aside
 The man who stands with arms akimbo set,
Until occasion tells him what to do;
 And he who waits to have his task marked out,
Shall die and leave his errand unfulfilled.
 Our time is one which calls for earnest deeds."
  —JAMES RUSSELL LOWELL.

IMPORTANCE OF EARNESTNESS

Not simply to the wind, however auspicious, does the seaman owe his progress. Without it, indeed, his ship would but rise and fall in the swell of the deep; but without the skill to catch and use the breeze, and compel it, even when adverse, by dexterous trimming of the yards, and setting of the sails, and handling of the helm, to force him on and over the waves, what service were the wind to him. So was it in Joseph's and so is it in all cases of success. God gives the opportunities; but success turns on the use we make of them; on the promptitude with which we seize the openings of providence; on the earnestness of character we bring into the field; on the resolution and energy we throw into our business.—GUTHRIE.

REWARDED ACCORDING TO EARNESTNESS

Our work does not amount to much. We only teach a class, or distribute a bundle of tracts, or preach a sermon, and we say, "Oh, if I had done it in some other way!" Christ will make no record of our bungling way if we only did the best we could. He will make a record of our intention and the earnestness of our attempt. We can not get the attention of our class, or we break down in out exhortation, or our sermon falls dead, and we go home disgusted and sorry; we try to speak, and feel Christ is afar off Why he is nearer than if we had succeeded, if we have been in earnest, for he knows we need sympathy, and he is touched with our infirmity.—TALMAGE.

EARNESTNESS IN PREACHING

According to my principles, if a man is a messenger of God, and knows that men are in danger, and believes that he is sent to rescue them, he must be lost in the enthusiasm of that work. Men often think that earnestness—excitement is dangerous. Yes; everything is dangerous in this world. From the time that a man is born into the world, until he leaves it, it is possible that danger may be coupled with everything he does. There is a danger that your feeling may be too boisterous, or of too coarse a nature, but there is no danger from excitement that is half so fearful as the danger of not feeling and not caring. A preacher who is earnest in everything he does, in all that he believes, and in all his movements, will generally carry the people with him.—BEECHER.

THE NEED OF EARNESTNESS

We lack men of apostolic zeal. Converted in a most singular way, by a direct interposition from heaven, Paul from that time forward became an earnest man. He had always been earnest, in his sins, and in his persecutions; but after he heard that voice from heaven, "Saul, Saul, why persecutest thou me?" and had received the mighty office of an apostle, and had been sent forth a chosen vessel unto the gentiles, you can scarcely conceive the deep, the awful earnestness he manifested. Whether he did eat, or drink, or whatsoever he did, he did all for the glory of his God. His zeal was so earnest that he could not restrain himself within a little sphere; but he preached the word everywhere. Where are the men like that man? He had a heart on fire.—SPURGEON.

EXAMPLE OF EARNESTNESS

When I was going to Europe in 1867, my Friend, Mr. Stuart, of Philadelphia, said, "Be sure to beat the General Assembly at Edinburg in June. I was there last year," he said, "and it did me a world of good." He said that a returned missionary was invited to speak to the General Assembly on the wants of India. This old missionary, after a brief address, told the pastors who were present to go home and stir up the churches to send young men to India to preach the Gospel. He spoke with such earnestness that after a while he fainted, and they carried him from the hall. When he recovered, he asked where he was, and they told him the circumstances under which he had been brought there. "Yes," he said, "I was making a plea for India, and I didn't quite finish my speech, did I?" After being told that he did not, he said, "Well, take me back and let me finish it." But they said, "No, you will die in the attempt." "Well," said he, "I will die if I don't," and the old man asked again that they would allow him to finish his plea. When he was taken back the whole congregation stood as one man, and as they brought him on the platform, with a trembling voice he said, "Fathers and mothers of Scotland, is it true that you will not let your sons go to India? I spent twenty-five years of my life there. I have come back with sickness, and shattered health. If it is true that we have no strong grandsons to go to India, I will pack up what I have and be off to-morrow, and I will let those heathen know that if I can not live for them, I can die for them." The world said that the old man was enthusiastic. in earnest, and that's what we want.—MOODY.

EDUCATION

"Wisdom is the principal thing: therefore get wisdom: and with all thy getting get understanding."—Prov. 4:7.

> "Knowledge and wisdom, far from being one,
> Have oft-times no connection, knowledge dwells
> In heads replete with thoughts of other men;
> Wisdom in minds attentive to their own.
> Knowledge is proud that he has learned so much,
> Wisdom humble that he knows no more."
> —WM. COWPER.

EDUCATION ALONE NOT ENOUGH

I heard two persons on the Wengern Alp talking by the hour together of the names of ferns; not a word about their characteristics, uses, or habits, but a medley of crack-jaw titles and nothing more. They evidently thought that they were ventilating their botany, and kept each other in countenance by alternate volleys of nonsense. Education alone is a branchless tree, and little worth. Knowledge lies not in mere words.—SPURGEON.

BIBLE A MEANS OF EDUCATION

God's word is a means of education for heaven. By His grace and your own cooperation, your soul may be gradually developed into a more perfect resemblance to Him. Finally your Heavenly Father will call you home, where you will see the angels and saints clothed in the beauty of Christ Himself, standing around His throne, and hear the word that will admit you into their society: "Well done." —MOODY.

EDUCATION IN CRIME

There is such a thing as education in crime. As there are medical schools for doctors, and commercial academies for merchants, so thieving is systematically taught in some of our large towns. One boy for instance gives this account of himself: "My father was a soldier and died when I was a little fellow, leaving mother very poor. She begged in the street for a living. She died about nine years ago. There was nobody to look after me. I soon fell among thieves, and was taken to Wentworth Street, in Whitechapel, to a house where I was boarded and lodged for six months, where I was taught to pick pockets. There were twenty more boys besides myself kept by a man and woman who got the plunder. Daily the woman dressed herself, put a bell in her pocket, also a purse. Any boy who could take the purse from her pocket without causing the bell to tinkle, got the money it contained. We stayed till we were well fitted to pick pockets." The extent to which this education is carried is almost incredible. What an argument for Christian mission schools!— GUTHRIE.

EDUCATION INCREASES RESPONSIBILITY

The educated rationalist may laugh at you. But to-morrow he will be trodden under foot, and will go down to shame and everlasting contempt. "Stop," you say, "suppose he graduated at Harvard? or at Princeton? or suppose he is at the head of one of the German Universities? I can not help that. God makes no special regulation for the graduates of Harvard or Princeton. Rejecting the Bible, they will go down to be companions of the most abandoned wretches in the universe, and more miserable than they, because of their superior education. One rule for all—for great brain and little brain; for high-foreheaded Greek professor, and for flat-skulled Esquimaux: "He that believeth and is baptized shall be saved; and he that believeth not shall be damned."—TALMAGE.

EDUCATION A FRUIT OF PAST INVESTIGATION

The wisdom of to-day is the fruit of the education of all past centuries. We are heirs to the accomplishments of forgotten ages. The knowledge we possess is as a tree which draws its life from the debris of forests that have crumbled into dust.—BEECHER.

EDUCATION FOSTERS MANHOOD

I plead for education, not because it is the highway to prosperity in law, or in medicine, or in the pulpit, or in political life, or in science, but because it means manhood. I plead for education as the indispensable condition of a continuing, complete, and perpetuated happiness.—IBID.

CHRISTIANITY AN EDUCATION

Christianity redeems us; not from sin only, but from all narrowness, meanness, and littleness of conception; it puts great thought into our hearts and bold words into our mouths, and leads us out from our village prisons to behold all nations of mankind. On this ground alone, Christianity is the best educator in the world. It will not allow the soul to be mean. It forces the heart to be noble and hopeful. It says, "Go and teach all nations;" "Go ye into all the world;" "Look not every man on his own things, but every man also on the things of others;" "Give and it shall be given unto you." It is something to have a voice so Divine ever stirring the will and mingling counsels. It is like a sea-breeze blowing over a sickly land; like sunlight piercing the fogs of a long dark night. If we have narrow sympathies, mean ideas, paltry conceptions, we are not scholars in the school of Christ We are citizens of the world; let us bring no reproach upon Christ by our exclusiveness.—PARKER.

ETERNITY

"The high and lofty One that inhabiteth eternity, whose name is Holy."—Isaiah 57:15.

"The bell strikes one. My hopes and fears
Start up alarmed, and o'er life's narrow verge
Look down—on what? A fathomless abyss!
A dread eternity! how surely mine!
And can eternity belong to me,
Poor pensioner on the bounties of an hour!"
—EDWARD YOUNG.

BUILDING FOR ETERNITY

Let us build for eternity. A ship, however pretty she may be, is not good for anything unless she can battle with the deep. It makes no difference how splendidly you build so far as this world is concerned, your life is a failure if you build not so that you can go out into the great future and make the harbor of eternal life. We are to live on. We are not to live again, but we are to live on without a break. Death is not an end. It is a new impulse. We are discharged out of this life, where we have been like arrows in a quiver. Death is a bow which shoots us into eternity.—BEECHER.

ETERNITY BEYOND COMPARISON

Afar off, one can hardly tell which is mountain and which is cloud. The clouds rise with peaks and summits, all apparently as solid, and certainly as glistening, as the snow-clad Alps, so that the clearest eye might readily be deceived. So do the things of time appear to De all important, far-reaching, and enduring, and eternal things are not always of equal weight to the soul with those near at hand. Yet, despite all our instinctive judgments may suggest to the contrary, nothing earthly can ever be lasting, nothing in time can be worth considering compared to eternity.—SPURGEON.

ETERNAL LIFE AND ETERNITY PARALLEL

Now when a man believes on the Lord Jesus Christ, he gets eternal life. A great many people make a mistake right there; he that believeth on the Son hath—h-a-t-h- hath eternal life; it does not say he shall have it when he comes to die; it is in the present sense; it is mine now—if I believe. You can't bury the gift of God; you can't bury eternal life, any more than you can bury eternity, for they are parallel.—MOODY.

ETERNITY WILL REVEAL TO SINNERS THEIR FOLLY

We are in darkness till we are converted; because we are blind—and that not by accident, but by nature—born blind. There are animals, both wild and domestic, which by a strange and mysterious law of Providence are in that state when born. "Having eyes, they see not." Apparently unripe for birth, they leave their mother's womb to pass the first period of their being utterly sightless. But when some ten days have come and gone, time unseals their eyelids, and they are delivered from the power of darkness. But not ten days, nor years, nor any length of time will do us any such friendly office. Not that we shall be always blind. Oh, how men shall see, and regret in another world, the folly they were guilty of in this! Eternity opens the darkest eyes, but opens them at last too late —GUTHRIE.

TIDES OF ETERNITY RISING

A gentleman wandering along on the beach of Scotland, where the high rocks came near the sea, was unmindful of the fact that the tide was rising, which would cut off his retreat. A man on the top of the rocks shouted, "Hallo! the tide is rising, and this is the last place through which you can make your escape; you had better climb up on to the rocks." The man laughed at the warning and went on. After awhile he thought it was time to return; he came back and found retreat cut off He tried to scale the rocks; he clambered half way up—could get no further. The wave came to his feet, came to his waist, came to his chin, and with a wild shriek for help he perished. Oh, brother, the tides of eternity are rising. Those only will be saved who get on the Rock of Ages.—TALMAGE.

FAITH

"Now faith is the substance of things hoped for, and the evidence of things not seen." —Hebrews 11:1

Of for a faith that will not shrink,
   Tho' pressed by every foe,
That will not tremble on the brink
   O' any earthly woe."

FAITH THE ONLY DOOR

There is only one door into heaven; that door is faith. There is only one ship that sails for the skies; her name is Faith. There is only one weapon with which to contend with opposition; that is faith. Faith is the first step; faith the second step; faith the third step; faith the fourth step; faith the last step. We enter the road by faith. We contend against adversaries by faith; we die by faith; heaven is the reward of faith.—TALMAGE.

FAITH TRIUMPHANT

May all of us have that faith in the Lord Jesus Christ which availeth, that faith which worketh by love, and so, though we have begun in the egg on earth, yet, through God's brooding, before we know it we shall chip the shell: and though we have lain so long coiled up and helpless, we shall begin to put forth plumes; and, disdaining the nest, and finding the ground chilly beneath our feet, with every gathering feather we shall pine for the air, and, pining, begin to try those notes which we are yet to learn; and, at length, in some bright and beaded morning, we shall spread our wings, and rising above the tangle and the thicket, soar through the blue, singing to the gate of heaven.—BEECHER.

AN EXAMPLE OF FAITH

Suppose a fire in the upper room of a house, and the people gathered in the street. A child is in the upper story: how is he to escape? He cannot leap down,—that were to be dashed to pieces. A strong man comes beneath, and cries, "Drop into my arms." It is a part of faith to know that the man is there; it is another part of faith to believe that the man is strong; but the essence of faith lies in dropping down into the man's arms. So, sinner, thou art to know that Christ died for sin; thou art also to understand that Christ is able to save, and thou art to believe that; but thou art not saved, unless, in addition to that, thou puttest thy trust in him to be thy Savior, and to be thine forever.—SPURGEON.

MORE FAITH

When we were in Edinburg, a man came to me and said, "Over yonder is one of the most prominent infidels in Edinburg. I wish you would go over and see him." I took my seat beside him and asked him if he was a Christian. He laughed at me, and said he didn't believe in the Bible. "Well," said I, after talking for sometime, "Will you let me pray with you?" "Yes," said he, "just pray, and see if God will answer your prayers." "Will you kneel?" "No, I won't kneel. Who be I going to kneel before?" He said it with considerable sarcasm. I got down and prayed beside the infidel. He sat up very straight so that the people would understand that he was not in sympathy with the prayer. After I got through, I said, "Well, my friend, I believe that God will answer my prayer, and I want you to let me know when you are saved." "Yes, I will let you know when I am saved," all with considerable sarcasm. At last up at Wick, at a meeting in the open air one night, on the outskirts of the crowd, I saw the Edingburg infidel. He said, "Didn't I tell you God wouldn't answer your prayer?" I said, "The Lord will answer my prayer yet." I had a few minutes conversation with him, and left him, and just a year ago this month, when we were preaching in Liverpool, I got a letter from one of the leading pastors of Edinburg, stating that that infidel had found his way to Christ.

There may be many in New York who will laugh at this idea, and say that God doesn't answer prayer, but He does, if Christians will only have faith.—What we want is to have more faith.—MOODY.

THE OLD AND THE NEW

Bring out from the dust of six thousand years the old covenant of Eden, and on that soiled and torn banner you read the fading motto, "Do and live." But what read we on the folds of this banner, which, defiant of hell and the world, waves above Calvary, and under which believers march to crowns and victory! The eye of a sinner's hope kindles at the sight of another and a better motto; for there, inscribed in the blood of Jesus, like red letters on a snow-white ground we read, "Believe and live." Salvation is the only thing needful for man, and faith is the one thing needful for salvation.—GUTHRIE.

HEAD-FAITH

Faith is practically nothing so long as it is merely in the head. Head faith can save no man. This is exactly so in daily life. There is no witchery nor mystery in this doctrine at all. Faith can not save you in commerce any more than it can save you in religion. Faith cannot save the body any more than it can save the soul.

A man believes that if he puts his money into certain funds, he will get back good interest with the most approved security, yet at the end of a year he gets literally nothing. How was that? Because, though he believed it, he did not put any money into the funds. Can faith save him? A man thoroughly believes that if he takes a certain mixture prescribed for him by good medical authority, he will get better, he will be recovered from his disease; but he gets no better; he gets worse; because, though he believed in the mixture, he did not take it. Can faith save him? A man wants to go to New York; he believes that ship is going; he is quite sure that that ship will be there in less than a fortnight; yet he himself will not be there! How is that? He had faith. He had not the shadow of a doubt. Yet there he is, in England! Can faith take him to New York? Can faith save him?— PARKER.

FORGIVENESS

"And forgive us our debts, as we forgive our debtors"—The Prayer of Prayers.

"When on the fragrant sandal tree,
    The woodman's ax descends,
And she who bloomed so beauteously
    Beneath the keen stroke bends,
E'en on the edge that brought her death,
Dying, she breathes her sweetest breath,
As if to token in her fall
"Peace to my foes, and love to all!"
How hardly man this lesson learns,
To smile, and bless the hand that spurns;
To see the blow, and feel the pain,
But render only love again!
This spirit ne'er was given on earth;
One had it,—He of heavenly birth;
Reviled, rejected, and betrayed,
No curse He breathed, no plaint He made,
But when in death's deep pang He sighed,
Prayed for his murderers and died."

CHRISTIANITY TEACHES FORGIVENESS

For though nature, fallen and unrenewed nature, hates her enemies, and, thirsting for vengeance, would drag them from the horns of the altar, Christianity embraces the bitterest foe in the arms of brotherhood.

Mercy, like the regions of space, has no limit; and as these stretch away before the traveler who looks out from the farthest star, so the loftiest intellect and the largest heart can descry no bounds to mercy. Like our Father in heaven, we are to forgive without stint, forgiving aa we expect to be forgiven.—GUTHRIE.

AN EXAMPLE OF FORGIVENESS

An old Christian black woman was going along the streets of New York with a basket of apples that she had for sale. A rough sailor ran against her and upset the basket, and stood back expecting to hear her scold frightfully; but she stooped down and picked up the apples, and said, "God forgive you, my son, as I do." The sailor saw the meanness of what he had done, felt in his pocket for his money, and insisted that she should take it all. Though she was black, he called her mother, and said, "Forgive me, mother; I will never do anything so mean again." Ah! there is a power in a forgiving spirit to overcome all hardness. There is no way of conquering men like that of bestowing upon them your pardon, whether they will accept it or not.—TALMAGE.

FORGIVENESS AND MEMORY

"I can forgive, but I cannot forget," is only another way of saying, "I will not forgive." A forgiveness ought to be like a cancelled note, tom in two and burned up, so that it can never be shown against the man.

HEDGE-HOG FORGIVENESS

There is an ugly kind of forgiveness in this world—a kind of hedge-hog forgiveness, shot out like quills. Men take one who has offended, and set him down before the blowpipe of their indignation, and scorch him, and burn his fault into him; and when they have kneaded him sufficiently with their fiery fists, then—they forgive him.— BEECHER.

CHRIST'S FORGIVENESS

In the midst of the darkness and the gloom of the cross, there came a voice from one of those thieves. It flashed into the soul of Jesus as He hung there, "This must be more than man; this must be the true Messiah." He cried out, "Lord remember me when Thou comest into Thy Kingdom!" We are anxious to get the last word or act of our dying friends. Here was the last act of Jesus. He snatched the thief from the jaws of death, saying, "This day shalt thou be with me in Paradise." Such was his forgiveness of sin, an act of grace, as his forgiveness of his murderers was an act of mercy.—MOODY.

WHO IS TO BEGIN?

Families and households often get awry. The younger brother differs from his elder brother,—sisters fall out. One wants more than belongs to him; another is knocked to the wall because he is weak; and there come into the heart bitterness and alienation, and often brothers and sisters have scarce a kind word to say of one another. Is it always to be so? Do not merely make it up, do not patch it up, do not cover it up,—go right down to the base. But who is to begin? I can tell you. You are! "But I am the eldest,"—yes, and therefore ought to begin. "But I am the youngest." Then why should the youngest be obstinate? Who are you that you should not go and throw yourself down at your brother's feet and say, "I have done you wrong, pardon me?" Who is to begin? You! Which? Both! When? Now!—PARKER.

FRIENDSHIP

"A man that hath friends must shew himself friendly: and there is a friend that sticketh closer than a brother."—Prov: 18:24.

> "For in companions
> That do converse and waste the time together,
> Whose souls do bear an equal yoke of love
> There must be needs a like proportion
> Of liniaments, of manners, and of spirit."
> —SHAKESPEARE. Merchant of Venice.

JESUS THE BEST FRIEND

I have found a great many kind friends but Jesus is the best. He understands me so well, and has such a way of putting up with my frailties, and has promised to do so much for me when all other loved ones swim away from my vision, and I can no more laugh with them over their joys or cry with them over their sorrows. Oh! when a man has trouble, he needs friends. When a man loses property, he needs all those of his acquaintances who have lost property to come in with their sympathy. When bereavement comes to a household, it is a comfort to have others who have been bereaved come in and sympathize. God is a sympathetic friend. O the tenderness of divine friendship.—TALMAGE.

FRIENDSHIP AND FAULTS

It is one of the severest tests of friendship to tell your friend of his faults. If you are angry with a man, or hate him, it is not hard to go to him and stab him with words, but so to love a man that you can not bear to see the stain of sin upon him, and to speak painful truth through loving words—that is friendship. But few have such friends. Our enemies usually teach us what we are at the point of the sword.—BEECHER.

SUFFERING FRIENDSHIP

In the French revolution, a young man was condemned to the guillotine, and shut up in one of the prisons. He was greatly loved by many, but there was one who loved him more than all put together. How know we this? It was his best earthly friend, his own father, and the love he bore the son was proven in this way: When the lists were called, the father, whose name was exactly the same as the son's, answered to the name, and the father rode in the gloomy tunebril out to the place of execution, and his head rolled beneath the axe instead of his son's, a victim to mighty love. See here an image of the love of Christ for sinners. "Greater love hath no man than this; that he laid down his life for his friends." But Jesus died for the ungodly! He is the friend of sinners. There is no friendship like Christ's.—SPURGEON.

FRIENDS MUST AGREE

Friends must agree. Enoch was a friend of God, as was Abraham. God and he agreed very well, so that at last God said to him, "come up here and walk with me." It is sweet to walk with God. We walk the wilderness today and the promised land to-morrow. Enoch found the right way, back there in that dim age; even so may we put our hands in God's hand and walk with Him as Enoch did, and commune with Him as friend with friend.— MOODY.

FRIENDSHIP PECULIAR TO MEN

Though the lower animals have feeling, they have no fellow-feeling. Have I not seen the horse enjoy his feed of corn, when his yoke-fellow lay dying in the neighboring stall, and never turn an eye of pity on the sufferer? They have strong passions, but no sympathy—no capacity for friendship. It is said that the wounded deer sheds tears; but it belongs to man only to weep with them that weep, and by sympathy divide another's sorrow and double another's joys. When thunder, following the dazzling flash has burst among our hills, when the horn of the Switzer has rung in his glorious valleys, when the boatman has shouted from the bosom of the rock-girt loch, wonderful were the echoes I have heard them make; but there is no echo so fine or wonderful as that which, in the sympathy of human hearts repeats the cry of another's sorrow, and makes me feel his pain almost as if it were my own.— GUTHRIE.

GOD

"The blessed and only Potentate, the King of kings, and Lord of lords: Who only hath immortality, dwelling in the light which no man can approach unto; whom no man hath seen, nor can see: to whom be honor and power everlasting."—1 Tim. 6:15.

"O Thou Eternal One! Whose presence bright
All space doth occupy, all motions guide—
Unchanged through time's all-devastating flight!
Thou only God—there is no God beside!
Being above all beings! Mighty one,
Whom none can comprehend and none explore!
Who fill'st existence with Thyself alone—
Embracing all, supporting, ruling o'er—
Being whom we call God, and know no more."
—GABRIEL DERZHAVIN.

GOD IS LOVE

Let no man, therefore, when he says, "Our Father which art in Heaven," suppose that he addresses a God without any color of strength, of equity, or of penalty. He is a God who loves you so that He will not suffer wickedness in you; and that if it be needful to purge wickedness out from you by exquisite pains, will employ the pains to purge it out. A God of love and justice will do that which is necessary to be done in order to redeem a soul from death; and whether pains and penalty will be now or hereafter, it will be averaged to the measure of necessity. The love of God does not take away the motive of fear, but augments it; it is a higher fear, it is a more generous fear. Love punishes. There is no punishment like that of love. And God is love. —BEECHER.

HIS NAME ETERNAL

God's name, like Himself is abiding. It is eternal. Even if the last harp of the glorified had been touched with the last fingers; if the last praise of the saints had ceased; if the last hallelujah had echoed through the then deserted vaults of Heaven, or they would be gloomy then; if the last immortal had been buried in his grave; if graves there might be for immortals-would the praise of His name cease then? No, by heaven! no; for yonder stand the angels; they too sing His glory; to Him the cherubim and seraphim do cry without ceasing, when they mention His name in that thrice holy chorus, "Holy, holy, holy, Lord God of armies." But if these where perished—if angels had been swept away, if the wing of seraph never flapped the ether, if the voice of cherub never sang his flaming sonnet, if the living creatures ceased their everlasting chorus, if the measured symphonies of glory were extinct in silence, would His name then be lost? Ah! no; for as God upon the throne He sits THE EVERLASTING ONE, the Father, Son and Holy Ghost.—SPURGEON.

WRONG CONCEPTION OF GOD

If I thought 1 could make the world believe that God is love, I would take that text and go up and down the earth, trying to counteract what Satan has been telling men—that God is not love. He has made the world believe it pretty 'effectually. It would not take twenty-four hours to make the world come to God, if you can only make them believe that God is love. If you have really made a man believe you love him, you have won him. But man has got a false idea about God, and will not believe He is a God of love. It is because he don't know Him. Whatever other conception of God, either right or wrong, you may have, don't let this be forgotten—He is love, love unchangeable, love everlasting, love unfailing.—MOODY.

GOD IN NATURE

Insects as well as angels, the flowers that spangle the meadow as well as the stars that spangle the sky, the lamp of the glow-worm as well as the light of the sun, the lark that sings in the air and the saint that sings in Paradise, the still small voice of conscience as well as the thunders that rend the clouds, or the trump that shall rend the tomb, these and all things else reveal God's attributes and proclaim his praise.—GUTHRIE.

GOD A PARENT

The Bible is a warm letter of affection from a parent to a child, yet there are many who see chiefly the severer passages. As there may be fifty or sixty nights of gentle dew in one summer, that will not cause as much remark as one hail-storm of half an hour, so there are those who are more struck with those passages of the Bible that announce the indignation of God than by those that announce his affection. God is a Lion, John says in the Book of Revelation. God is a Breaker, Micah announces in his prophecy. God is a Rock. God is a King. But hear also that God is Love. A father and his child are walking out in the fields on a summer's day, and there comes up a thunder storm; and there is a flash of lightning that startles the child, and the father says, "My dear, that is God's eye" There comes a peal of thunder and the father says, "My dear that is God's voice" But the clouds go off the sky, and the storm is gone, and the light floods the heavens, and floods the landscape; and the father forgets to say, "That is God s smile." Let us not shut our eyes to God's, tender nature. He is a father. He is our mother.—TALMAGE.

A CHALLENGE TO ATHEISTS

You say this God was dreamed by human genius. Be it so. Make Him a creature of fancy. What then? The man who made, or dreamed, or otherwise projected such a God must be the author of some other work of equal or approximate importance. Produce it! That is the sensible reply to so bold a blasphemy. Singular if man has made Jehovah and then has taken to the drudgery of making oil paintings, and ink poems, and huts to live in. Where is the congruity. A man says he kindled the sun, and when asked for his proof, he strikes a match which the wind blows out! Is the evidence sufficient? Or a man says he has covered the earth with all the green and gold of summer, and, when challenged to prove it, he produces a wax flower which melts in his hands! Is the proof convincing? The God of the Bible calls for the production of other gods—gods wooden, gods stony, gods ill-bred, gods well-shaped, and done up skillfully for market uses; from His Heavens He laughs at them, and from His high throne he holds them in derision. Again and again I demand that the second effort of human genius bear some obvious relation to the first. We wait for the evidence. We insist upon having it; and, that we may not waste our time in idle expectancy, we will meanwhile call upon God, saying, "Our Father who art in Heaven, hallowed be Thy name. Thy will be done in earth, as it is in Heaven!"—PARKER.

THE GOSPEL

"I am not ashamed of the Gospel of Christ: for it is the power of God unto salvation, to every one that believeth."—Rom. 1:16.

"Upon the Gospel's sacred page
The gathered beams of ages shine;
And as it hastens every age
But makes its brightness more divine.
—SIR JOHN BOWRING.

THE GOSPEL ETERNAL

When was there a time when the Gospel of Christ did not exist? Can you point your finger to 'a period when the religion of Jesus was an unheard of thing? "Yes," one replies, "before the days of Christ and his apostles." But we answer, "Nay, Bethlehem was not the birthplace of the gospel. Though Jesus was born there, there was a gospel long before the birth of Jesus, and a preached one, too; although not preached in its simplicity and plainness, as we hear it now. There was a gospel in the wilderness of Sinai, although it might be confused with the smoke of the incense, and only to be seen through slaughtered victims; yet there was a gospel there." Yea, more, we take them back to the fair trees of Eden, where the fruits perpetually ripened, and summer always rested, and amid these groves we tell them there was a gospel, and we let them hear the voice of God as he spoke to recreant man, and said, "The seed of the woman shall bruise the serpent's head." Such was the beginning of the gospel— SPURGEON.

GOSPEL MEANT FOR ALL

"The Spirit of the Lord is upon me because He hath anointed me to preach the Gospel." Now, the question is, who shall the Gospel be preached to? There is a certain class of people who think that the Gospel is very good for drunkards, and thieves, and vagabonds; but there are so many of these self-righteous Pharisees to-day, who are drawing their filthy rags of self-righteousness around them, and thinking the Bible is for a certain class. If I understand it correctly, the Gospel is for all. There is no distinction; rich and poor must be served alike; learned and unlearned, all have to come into the Kingdom of God one way, and that is by believing the Gospel of Jesus Christ —MOODY.

THE GOSPEL DESTINED TO BE UNIVERSAL

A single grain of corn would, were the produce of each season sown again, so spread from field to field, from country to country, from continent to continent, as in the course of a few years to cover the face of the whole earth with one wide harvest, employing all the sickles, filling all the barns, and feeding all the mouths in the world. Such an event, indeed, could not happen in nature, because each latitude has its own productions, and there is no plant formed to grow alike under the sun of Africa, and amid the snows of Greenland. It is the glory of the Gospel, and one of the evidences of its divine origin that it can; and, unless prophecy fail, that it shall. There is not a shore which shall not be sown with this seed; not a land but shall yield harvests of glory to God and of souls for heaven. By revolutions that are overturning all things, by war's rude and bloody share, and otherwise, God is breaking up the fallow ground, and ploughing the earth for a glorious seed-time. The seed that sprang up in Bethlehem shall wave over Arctic snows and desert sands; and as every shore is washed by one sea, and every land that lies between the poles is girdled by one hemisphere, and every drop of blood in human veins belongs to one great family of brothers, so in God's set time, men of every color and tongue shall cherish a common faith, and trust in a common Savior.—GUTHRIE.

THE GOSPEL A DELUSION

Some accuse the Gospel of being a delusion. Powerful delusion, all-conquering delusion, earth-quaking delusion of the Christian religion. Yea, it goes on, it is so impertinent, and it is so overbearing, this chimera of the

Gospel, that it has conquered the great picture galleries of the world, the old masters and the young masters, and having done this it is not satisfied until it has conquered the music of the world. Yes this chimera of the Gospel is not satisfied until it goes on and builds itself into the most permanent architecture, so it seems as if the world is never to get rid of it. What are some of the finest buildings in the world? St. Paul's, St. Peter's, the churches and cathedrals of all Christendom. Yes, this impertinence of the Gospel, this vast delusion is not satisfied until it projects itself, and in one year gives, contributes $6,250,000 to foreign missions. The work of which is to make dunces and fools on the other side of the world—people we have never seen.—TALMAGE.

THE GOSPEL AT HOME

Spreading Christianity abroad is sometimes an excuse for not having it at home. A man may cut grafts from his tree till the tree itself has no top left with which to bear fruit In the end, the power of Gospel missions will

be measured by the zeal of enlightened piety at home, as the circulation of the blood at the extremities of the body will depend upon the soundness of the lungs and heart. I do not say that we should not send the Gospel abroad; but that we may do it, there must be more of it at home. We must deepen the wells of salvation, or drawing will run them dry.—BEECHER.

GRACE

"The grace of God that bringeth salvation."—Titus 2:11.

"Thou art coming to a king!
Large petitions with thee bring,
For His grace and power are such,
Thou canst never ask too much."

LAW AND GRACE

How differently do law and grace work! The law say "Stone the sinner;" grace says, "Forgive him." When Moses was in Egypt to punish Pharaoh, he turned the waters into blood. When Christ was on earth, He turned the water into wine. That is the difference between law and grace. Law makes us crooked; grace straightens us. The law makes us vile; grace cleanses us. When the law came out of Horeb, 3,000 men were lost. At Pentecost, under grace, 3,000 men got life. What a difference! When Moses came up to the burning bush, he was commanded to take the shoes off from his feet. When the prodigal came home after sinning, he was a given a pair of shoes to put on his feet. I would a thousand times rather be under grace than under the law.—MOODY.

GRACE OF GOD AN ARCH

As with an arch, the grace of God stands the firmer the more weight you lay on it; it's sufficiency, at least, will be the more evident; the more clearly you will see the promise, "My grace is sufficient for thee." With the well ever full and ever flowing, our vessels need never be empty. Whether, therefore you want more faith, more purity of heart or peace of mind, more light or love, a humbler or a holier spirit, a calmer or a tenderer conscience, a livelier sense of Christ's excellences or of your own unworthiness, more tears for Christ's feet, or honor for his head, fear pot to draw, to hope, to ask too much.—GUTHRIE.

GRACE DOES NOT CHANGE MEN FROM NATURE

The popular impression is that grace is designed to change men from nature. No. They are sinful simply because they have deviated from their true nature, or fallen short of it. Grace is given to bring out the followers of every man's nature. Not the nature which schoolmen write about; but that nature which God thought of, when He put forth man, and pronounced him a child of God, bearing his Father's likeness.—BEECHER.

EARLY TRAINING

Grace, like flower-seed needs to be sown in spring. The first fifteen years of life, and often the first six, decide the eternal destiny.

CHRIST ON A THRONE OF GRACE

Christ is on a throne of grace. Our case is brought before him. The question is asked: "Is there any good about this man?" The law answers, "None." Justice says, "None." Nevertheless Christ hands over our pardon, and asks us to take it. Oh! The height and depth, the length and breadth of his mercy.—TALMAGE.

PAYSON ON "GRACE"

Payson, when dying, expressed himself with great earnestness respecting the grace of God as exercised in saving lost men, and seemed particularly affected that it should be bestowed on one so ill-deserving as himself. "O, how sovereign! O, how sovereign! Grace is the only thing that can make us like God. I might be dragged through heaven, earth, and hell, and I should be the same sinful, polluted wretched transgressor, unless God himself should renew and cleanse me."—SPURGEON.

HEAVEN

"There remaineth therefore a rest for the people of God"—Heb. 4:9.

Jerusalem the golden,
With milk and honey blessed,
Beneath thy contemplation
Sink heart and voice oppressed,
I know not, O I know not
What social joys are there;
What radiance of glory
What light beyond compare.
—BERNARD of Cluny, Tr. by J. M. NEALE.

HEAVEN A PLACE OF LOVE

Heaven is the only place where the conditions of love can be fulfilled. There it is essentially mutual. Everybody loves everybody else. In this world of wickedness and sin it seems impossible to be all on a perfect equality. When we meet people who are bright and beautiful and good, we have no difficulty in loving them. All the people of heaven will be like that. There will be no fear of misplaced confidence there. We will never be deceived by those we love. When a suspicion of doubt fastens upon any one who loves, their happiness from that moment is at an end. There will be no suspicion there.

"Beyond these chilling winds and gloomy skies,
Beyond death's cloudy portal,
There is a land where beauty never dies,
Where love becomes immortal."
—MOODY.

COMFORT FOR SORROWFUL HEARTS

Oh ye whose locks are wet with the dews of the night of grief; ye whose hearts are heavy because those well-known footsteps sound no more at the doorway, yonder is your rest! There is David triumphant; but once he bemoaned Absalom. There is Abraham enthroned; but once he wept for Sarah. There is Paul, he is exultant, but he once sat with his feet in the stocks. There is Payson radiant with immortal health; but on earth he was always sick. No toil: no tears: no partings: no strife: no agonizing cough: no night. No storm to ruffle the crystal sea. No alarm to strike from the cathedral towers. No dirge throbbing from seraphic hearts. No tremor in the everlasting song; but rest—perfect rest—unending rest.— TALMAGE.

THE SWEETEST MUSIC

The sweetest music is not the peal of marriage bells, nor tender descants in moonlight woods, nor trumpet notes of victory—it is the soul's welcome to heaven. God grant that, when we die there may not come booming to our ear the dreadful sound, "Depart!" But may we hear stealing upon the air the mellow chime of all the celestial bells saying, "Come, come, come, ye blessed, enter ye into the joy of your Lord!"

JOY FOR TIMID SAINTS

To a Christian who has lived all his lifelong in bondage unto fear, not daring to believe himself a child of God, how sweet will be the awakening in heaven. With great dread and trembling he will approach the death hour, and go down through chilling mists and vapors to the unknown and when upon the other shore sweet strains come to his ear, he will not understand them, but fair form after fair form will appear to greet him, and at length, from the impearled atmosphere God's whole band of gathering and reaping angels, more in number than the autumn leaves out-streaming from the forest when there are bursts of wind, will come forth, filling all the air with music, and minister unto him an abundant entrance into the kingdom! It were almost enough to make one's heaven to stand and see the first wild stirring of joy in the face, and hear the first rapturous cry as they cross the threshold, of thousands of timid Christians who lived weeping and died sighing, but who will wake to find every tear an orb of joy and every sigh an inspiration of God. O, the wondrous joy of heaven to those who did not expect it!—BEECHER.

THE CHRISTIANS HOME

In his best hours, home, his own sinless home—a home with his Father above that starry sky—will be the wish of every Christian man. He looks around him—the world is full of suffering; he is distressed by its sorrows, and vexed by its sins. He looks within him—he finds much in his own corruptions to grieve him. In the language of a heart repelled, grieved, vexed, he often turns his eye upward, saying, "I would not live alway." No. Not for all the gold of the world's mines, not for all the pearls of the seas, not for all the pleasures of her flashing, frothy cup, not for all the crowns of her kingdoms—would I live here alway. Like a bird about to migrate to those sunny lands where no winter sheds her snows, or strips the grove, or binds the dancing streams, he will often in spirit be pruning his wing for the hour of his flight to glory. —GUTHRIE.

HEAVEN WORTH STRIVING FOR

Julius Caesar, going towards Rome with his army, and hearing that the senate and people had fled from it, said, "They that will not fight for this city, what city will they fight for?" If we will not take pains for the Kingdom of heaven, what kingdom will we take pains for?—SPURGEON.

HELPS ON THE WAY

When Abraham went from Ur of the Chaldees at the command of God, on his way he received a renewal of the promise. Very beautiful was this! It showed that he was on the right road, and that God's faithfulness followed him like an angel of defence. It is so with ourselves on the journey to the better Canaan, where the upper springs never dry, and the summer lies like an infinite blessing over the whole land.

> "There shall be no more snow,
> No weary wandering feet."

O, fair Canaan! A land so near, did we but know it! Just over the river, the stream, the faint dark rill. It was a river to our youth, it is a stream to our manhood, it will be but a rill to the faith of our old age! And as we move to it, step by step, what words of love and hope are spoken to us by the Lord of the fair land! How he helps us up the steps that are long and hard; how he cheers us along the road that is flat and tedious; how he throws a robe around us when the fierce winds blow upon us in bitter cold.—PARKER.

HOLINESS

"Holiness to the Lord."—Ex. 28:36.

"More holiness give me,
  More strivings within;
More patience in suff'ring,
  More sorrow for sin,
More faith in my Savior,
  More sense of His care;
More joy in His service,
  More purpose in prayer."

A HOLY MAN

Abraham was a holy man. Each important transaction of life was entered on in a pious spirit, and hallowed by religious exercises. His tent was a moving temple. His household was a pilgrim church. Wherever he rested, whether by the venerable oak of Mamre, or on the olive slopes of Hebron, or on the lofty forest-crowned ridge of Bethel, an altar arose; and his prayers went up with its smoke to heaven. Such daily, intimate and loving communion did this grand saint maintain with heaven, that God calls him his "friend." He lived on terms of fellowship with God, such as had not been seen since the days of Eden. Voices addressed him from the skies; angels paid visits to his tent, and visions of celestial glory hallowed his lowly couch and mingled with his nightly dreams. His life was one of holy devotion and consecrated righteousness.—GUTHRIE.

HOLINESS BY THE BLOOD

Holiness is gained only by the application of Christ's blood. A heathen got worried about his sins, and came to a priest and asked how he might be cured. The priest said, "If you will drive spikes in your shoes and walk five hundred miles you will get over it." So he drove spikes in his shoes and began the pilgrimage, trembling, tottering, agonizing on the way, until he got about twenty miles and sat down under a tree, exhausted. Near by, a missionary was preaching Christ, the Savior of all men. When the heathen heard it, he pulled off his sandals, threw them as far as he could, and cried, "That's what I want; give me Jesus! give me Jesus!" Oh, ye who have been convicted and worn of sin, trudging on all your days to reap eternal woe, will you not, at the announcement of a full and glorious atonement, throw your torturing transgressions to the wind? "The blood of Jesus Christ cleanseth from all sin."—TALMAGE.

A BEAUTIFUL CHARACTER

Holiness is beauty. There is no beauty like that of a pure character. The grandest sight on this earth is not the march of the all-conquering storm whose cloudy battalions go rushing through the sounding heavens; the most beautiful thing on earth is not the garden which opens, and sends forth from its censers fragrance; it is not the stateliness of the tree which you sit under through the long summer's day; those are not the most beautiful things on earth that art carves out of stone; the beauty of the soul lies in its secret chambers; and the rich, deep, just, holy and loving natures—these are the beautiful thing's of this world. There is nothing so beautiful as Christ in man.— BEECHER.

ACQUIRED BY COMMUNION WITH CHRIST

As courtiers are more polite in their manners than ordinary subjects, because they are more in their prince's company, so may the society of the Lord's holy servants raise the tone of our thought and make us aspire after a sanctity beyond what we possess. If the society of Christ's disciples be thus helpful, we may be sure that communion with their Lord will be still more so. If we learn good manners from the man, what may we expect from being with the master. From Jesus we shall learn gentleness and love, purity and self-sacrifice, and so acquire the courtly manners of the Prince of Peace. There is no preparation for heaven like abiding with heaven's Lord. The oftener we are in God's court, the more holy we shall become.—SPURGEON.

HOLINESS AND HUMILITY

Some one asked a minister if he had ever received a second blessing since he was converted. "What do you mean?" was the reply. "I have received ten thousand since the first." A great many think because they have been holy once, they are going to be holy for all time after. But O, my friends, we are leaky vessels, and have to be kept right under the fountain all the time in order to be kept full. If we are going to be used by God, we must be very humble. Humility and holiness go together. A man that lives close to God will be the humblest of men. Let us keep near Him.—MOODY.

HOLY SPIRIT

"He shall baptize you with the Holy Ghost, and with fire."— Matt. 3:11.

"Our blessed Redeemer, ere he breathed
His tender last farewell.
A Guide, a Comforter bequeathed,
With us on earth to dwell."
-HARRIET AUBER.

THE SPIRIT ABOVE

In the far East there is a bird called the Huma, about which is the beautiful superstition that upon whatever head the shadow of that bird rests, upon that head there shall be a crown. Oh, thou Dove of the Spirit, floating above us, let the shadow of thy wing fall upon our heads, that each, at last, in heaven may wear a crown! a crown! and hold in his right hand a star! a star!—TALMAGE.

NECESSARY TO CONVERSION

Some regard religion as a sort of divine aura, which descends upon a man and encircles him, as silvery mists enwreath autumnal mountain tops. There is a sense in which this is true. No one would become a Christian without the direct aid of the Holy Spirit, any more than a bud would become a blossom without the influence of the sun; but yet personal religion is the result of personal choice.—BEECHER.

THE OFFICE OF THE SPIRIT

Call it fanaticism if you will, but I trust that there are some of us who know what it is to be always, or generally, under the influence of the Holy Spirit—always in one sense, generally in another. When we have difficulties we ask the direction of the Holy Ghost. When we do not understand a portion of Holy Scripture, we ask God the Holy Ghost to shine upon us. When we are depressed, the Holy Spirit comforts us. You can not tell what the power of the indwelling of the Holy Ghost is. How it pulls back the hand of the saint when he would touch the forbidden thing; how it prompts him to make a covenant with his eyes; how it binds his feet lest they should fall in a slippery 'way; how it restrains his heart, and keeps him from temptation. O ye, who know nothing of the indwelling of the Holy Ghost, despise it not—SPURGEON.

A REPROVER OF SIN

The Holy Spirit tells a man of his faults in order to lead him to a better life. In John 14:8, we read: "He is to reprove the world of sin." There is a class of people who don't like this part of the Spirit's work. Do you know why? Because He convicts them of sin; they don't like that. What they want is some one to speak comforting words and make everything pleasant; keep everything all quiet; tell them there is peace when there is war; tell them it is light when it is dark; tell them everything is growing better; that the world is getting on amazingly in goodness; that is the kind of preaching they are seeking for. That suits human nature, for it is frill of pride. Men will strut around and say, "Yes, I believe that; the world is improving; I am a good deal better man than my father was; my father was too strict; he was Puritanical. O, we are getting on; we are more liberal; my father wouldn't think of going out riding on Sunday, but we will; we will trample the laws of God under our feet; we are better than our fathers."

Just wait till you bring the Word of God to bear upon them, and the Spirit drives it home, then men will say: "I don't like that kind of preaching; I will never go to hear that man again." The Spirit of God convicts men of sin. Do not blame the preacher for it, but the Holy Ghost.—MOODY.

THE SPIRIT'S POWER

Sin never wove, in hottest hell-fires the devil never forged, a chain, which the Spirit of God, wielding the hammer of the word, cannot strike from fettered limbs. Put that to the test. Try the power of prayer. Let continued, constant, earnest, wrestling prayer be made for those that are chained to their sins, and, so to speak, "thrust into the inner prison," and see, as when on that night when Peter was led forth by the angels' hand, whether your prayers are not turned into most grateful praises.—GUTHRIE.

HOME

"And the Lord hath brought me home again."—Ruth 1:21.

"I was a wandering sheep
 I did not love the fold;
I did not love my shepherd's voice,
 I would not be controlled:
I was a wayward child,
 I did not love my home,
I did not love my Father's voice —
 I loved afar to roam.

No more a wandering sheep,
 I love to be controlled,
I love my tender shepherd's voice,
 I love the peaceful fold:
No more a wayward child,
 I seek no more to roam;
I love my heavenly Father's voice,
 I love, I love His home."

WHAT IT MEANS

Home—ask ten different men the meaning of that word and they will give you ten different definitions. To one it means love at the hearth, it means plenty at the table, industry at the workstand, intelligence at the books, devotion at the altar. In that home, Discord never sounds his warwhoop, and Deception never tricks with his false face. To him it means a greeting at the door and a smile at the chair. Peace hovering like wings, joy clapping her hands with laughter. Life a tranquil lake. Pillowed on the ripples sleep the shadows.

Ask another man "What is home?" He will tell you it is Want looking out of a cheerless fire grate, kneading hunger in an empty bread tray. The damp air shivering with curses. No Bible on the shelf. Children, robbers and murderers in embryo. Obscene songs their lullaby. Every face a picture of ruin: want in the background, and sin staring from the front. No Sabbath wave rolling over that door-sill. Vestibule the pit. Shadow of infernal walls. Furnace for forging everlasting chains. Faggots for an unending funeral pile. Awful word! It is spelled with curses, it weeps with ruin, it chokes with woe, it sweats with the death agony of despair. The word "home" in the one case means everything bright. The word "home" in the other case means everything terrific. —TALMAGE.

HOTEL VERSUS HOME

A man living at a hotel is like a grape-vine in a flower pot—moveable, carried around from place to place, docked at the root and short at the top. No where can a man get real root-room, and spread out his branches until they touch the morning and the evening, but in his own home. —BEECHER.

GOING HOME

See how the horse pricks up his ears and quickens his pace when you turn his head to his stable. Much more then should intelligent Christian men feel the attractions of their heavenly home. Courage, brothers and sisters; we, too, are homeward bound. Every hour brings us nearer to the many mansions. We are not going from home, or we might hang our heads: our way is toward the Father's house on high, therefore let us rejoice at every step we take.—SPURGEON.

MAKING A HOME HAPPY

A little girl who had attended one of our meetings went home and climbed upon her father's knees and said, "Papa, you have been drinking again." It troubled him. If his wife had spoken to him, he might have got mad and gone out into some shop or saloon, and got more liquor, but that little child acted like an angel. He came down to our meetings with her and found out how he might be saved, and now that home is a little heaven. There are many homes that might be made happy in that way.— MOODY.

HOPE

"For we are saved by hope."—Rom. 8:24.

"Hope, only hope, of all that clings
Around ns, never spreads her wings."
—O. W. HOLMES.

HOPELESS SOULS

While some saints enjoy a clear assurance of their salvation, and stretching toward heaven behold the land that is very far off, as seamen from their outlook descry the mountain-tops, when their bark is ploughing a waste of waters, and yet a long way from land, there are other Christians who pass their days in a state of despondency. The sun seldom breaks out to cheer them. Their hope has a hard fight with their fears. It is little they know of rejoicing in the Lord, and joy in the God of their salvation. By help of God's word, their compass, they succeed, no doubt, in steering their way to heaven, but it is over a troubled sea, and under a cloudy sky; nor are they ever happy enough to be delivered from doubt and fear, till fears are lost in light, and they find themselves safe in glory.—GUTHRIE.

THE STAR OF HOPE

Christ is the star of hope. I would like to have my death-bed under that star—I would like to have my eye on that star, so I could be assured of the morning. Then the dash of the surf on the sea of death would only be the billowing up of the promise, "When thou passest through the waters I will be with thee, and the rivers, they shall not overflow thee." All other lights will fail, the light that falls from the scroll of fame, the light that flashes from the gem in the beautiful apparel, the light that flames from the burning lamps of a banquet—but this light bums on and bums on. Paul kept his eye on that star until he could say, "I have fought the good fight, I have finished my course, I have kept the faith." Edward Payson kept his eye on that star until he could say, "The breezes of heaven fan me." John Tennant kept his eye on that star until he could say, "Welcome, sweet Lord Jesus, welcome, eternity." No other star ever pointed a mariner into so safe a harbor. No other star ever sunk its silver anchor so deep into the waters.—TALMAGE.

A CHAMBER OF THE SOUL

Hope is one of the chambers of the soul—if haply you can see the inscription over the door. It has two sides and two windows. From one of these you can see the stars, the heaven beyond, the Holy City, the angels of God, the General Assembly, and church of the first-born. This is shut! The other window looks out into the world's highway, and sees men, caravans, artificers, miners, artisans, engineers, builders, bankers, brokers, pleasure-mongers. That window stands wide open, and is much used!—BEECHER.

NO WORD FOR HOPE

It is reported that in the Tamul language there is no word for hope. Alas! poor men, if we were all as destitute of the blessed comfort itself, as these Tamul speakers are of the word! What must be the misery of souls in hell, where they remember the word, but can never know hope itself!—SPURGEON.

NECESSITY OF HOPEFULNESS

Did you ever notice this, that no man or woman is ever used by God to build up His kingdom who has lost hope? Now, I have been observing this through different parts of the country, and wherever I have found a worker in God's vineyard who has lost hope, I have found a man or woman not very useful. Now, just look at these workers. Let your mind go over the past for a moment Can you think of a man or woman whom God has used to build His kingdom who has lost hope? I don't know of any; I never heard of such an one. It is very important to have hope in the Church, and it is the work of the Holy Ghost to impart hope, "that you may abound in hope through the power of the Holy Ghost." A map filled with the Spirit of God will be very hopeful—MOODY.

HUMILITY

"He that humbleth himself shall be exalted."—Matt. 18:4.

"Higher than the highest heaven,
Deeper than the deepest sea.
Lord, Thy love at last has conquered,
None of self, and all of Thee."

THE CHILD OF KNOWLEDGE

Wise men ever know their own ignorance and are ready to learn. Humility is the child of knowledge. Michael Angelo was found by the Cardinal Farnese walking in solitude amid the ruins of the Coliseum, and when he expressed his surprise, the great artist answered, "I go yet to school that I may continue to learn." Who among us can after this, talk of finishing our education? We have need to learn of all around us. He must be very foolish who cannot tell us something; or more likely, we must be very foolish not to be able to learn of him.—SPURGEON.

GOD'S ALPHABET

I suppose Isaiah thought be was as good as most men, in his day, and perhaps he was a good deal better than most men, but when he saw the Lord, he cried, "Woe is me, for I am undone; because I am a man of unclean lips". When he saw the Lord, he saw his own deformity, and he fell in the dust before the Lord. And that is the proper place for the sinner. Until men realise their own uncleanness they talk of their own righteousness, but the moment they catch a sight of Him their mouth is stopped. We can not learn to read till we learn the alphabet We can not come into His kingdom until we are humble. That is God's alphabet —MOODY.

THE STRENGTH OF PIETY

We have wondered at the lowliness of a man, who stood among his compeers like Saul among the people—to find him simple, gentle, generous, docile, humble as a little child—till we found that it is with great men as with great trees. What giant tree has not giant roots? When the tempest has blown over some such monarch of the forest, and he lies in death stretched out at his full length upon the ground, on seeing the mighty roots that fed him—the strong cables that moored him to the soil—we cease to wonder at his noble stem, and the broad, leafy, lofty head he raised to heaven, defiant of storms. Let us not forget that humility is the root and strength of lofty piety.—GUTHRIE.

SONS OF HUMANITY

They who have been the deliverers of literature and nations have come from homes without affluence, and by the discipline of their own privations have learned how to speak and fight for the ignorant and oppressed. Poetry and science and laws and constitutions and commerce were born, like Jesus, in a manger. Most of the great thoughts which have seemed the axletrees on which the centuries turned, had their start in obscure corners, and had Herods who tried to slay them, and Iscariots who betrayed them, and unjust prelates who condemned them, and rabbles that crucified them, till they burst out again in glorious resurrection. Many are the noble sons of humanity.—TALMAGE.

JOY A FRUIT OF HUMILITY

Our humiliations work out our most elevated joys. The way that a drop of rain comes to sing in a leaf that rustles in the top of a tree all summer long, is by going down to the roots first, and from thence ascending to the bough.— BEECHER.

INFIDELITY

"Without God in the world."—Eph. 2:12.

God is in this and every place;
    But O, how dark and void
To me!—'tis one great wilderness
    This earth without my God."
        —CHARLES WESLEY.

Forth from his dark and lonely hiding place,
    Portentious sight! the owlet Atheism,
Sailing on obscene wings athwart the noon,
    Drops his blue-fringed lids, and holds them close,
And hooting at the glorious sun in heaven,
    Cries out, Where is it?
        —COLERIDGE.

THE MOST ALARMING INFIDELITY

The most dangerous infidelity of the day is the infidelity of rich and orthodox churches.—BEECHER.

HAVE INFIDELS SOMETHING BETTER?

No matter how infidel philosophers may regard the Bible; they may say that Genesis is awry, and that the Psalms are more than half bitter imprecations, and the Prophecies only the phantasies of brain-bewildered men, and the Gospels weak laudations of an impostor, and the Epistles but the letters of a mad Jew, and that the whole book has had its day; I shall cling to it until they show me a better revelation. The Bible emptied, effete, worn out! 1/ all the wisest of the world were placed man to man, they could not sound the shallowest depth of the Gospel of John. O philosophers! break the shell, and fly out, and let me hear how you can sing. Not of passion—I know that already; not of wordly power—I hear that everywhere; but teach me, through your song, how to find joy in sorrow, strength, in weakness, and light in darkest days; how to bear buffeting and scorn, how to welcome death, and to pass through its ministration into the sphere of life; and this not for me only, but for the whole world that groans and travails in pain; and until you can do this, speak not to me of a better revelation.—IBID.

INFIDELITY A SIN

I affirm, and the world declares it, unbelief is a sin. Is it not a sin for a creature to doubt the word of its maker? Is it not a crime and an insult to the Divinity for me, an atom, a particle of dust, to dare to deny His words? Is it not the very summit of arrogance and extremity of pride, for a son of Adam to say, even in his heart, "God, I doubt thy grace; I doubt thy love; I doubt thy power?" Oh! sirs, believe me, could you roll all sins into one mass; could you take murder, and blasphemy, and lust, and adultery and everything that is vile, and unite them all into one vast globe of black corruption, they would not equal then, the sin of unbelief. This is the monarch sin, the quintessence of guilt; the mixture of the venom of all crimes; the dregs of the wine of Gomorrah; it is the masterpiece of Satan; the chief work of the devil.—SPURGEON.

INFIDELS IGNORANT OF THE BIBLE

Of all the skeptics and infidels I have ever met, I have yet to meet the first one that has read the Bible through from beginning to end. Now, if a book comes out, and) you have not read all of it, you say, "I have not read it through yet, and don't like to express my opinion until I have more carefully read it." But people are not afraid of expressing their opinion of God's book after having read a few chapters, and because they don't understand what they have read, they condemn the whole. When these infidels and unbelievers go up and stand before the Lord, they will say, "I was very anxious to accept your invitation to attend the marriage supper of the Lamb, but there were some things in the Bible that were dark and mysterious, and so I could not accept the invitation." That excuse sounds very well here, but up there you can't tell that. You will be speechless when you stand before God's bar.—MOODY.

INFIDELITY DEFEATED

The history of infidelity, were it written, would present a succession of ignominious defeats; defeats due not to any want of ability in those who have assailed the truth, but to this: that its defenders have driven them out of all their positions. The history, the morality, the theology, the consistency, the authenticity, the genuineness of the Bible, the truth of its prophecies, and the very possibility of its miracles have been all attacked, each in its turn, and with the same result. We have seen the soldier return from the fields of war with scars as well as medals on his breast, but our religion has come out of a thousand fights unscarred, from a thousand fires unscathed. She bears no more evidence of the assaults she has sustained than the air of the swords that have cloven it, or the sea of the keels which have ploughed its foaming waves; than some bold rooky headland of the billows that dashing against it in proud but impotent fury, have shivered themselves on its sides.— GUTHRIE.

A WORD TO MR. INGERSOLL

He (Mr. Ingersoll) is said to be a very brave man. I dare him to do one thing. I dare him to take his mother's Bible, and some Sunday afternoon, go into his room, and locking the door, kneel down, and while kneeling read the fourteenth chapter of John. Nothing there about Jonah and the whale; nothing there about the sun and moon stopping; nothing there about the manner in which Eve was made. Certainly a man so brave that he defies the God of the universe, and scoffs at the armies of martyrs and apostles, and prophets, and bullies perdition—certainly, a man as brave as that ought to be brave enough on a Sabbath afternoon to go into his room and kneel down, if the door is locked, and read the fourteenth chapter of John.

Here is infidelity: no prayer on her lips, no benediction on her brow, both hands clenched—what for? To fight Christianity. That is the entire business. That is the complete mission of infidelity—to fight Christianity. Where are her schools, her colleges, her asylums of mercy? Let me throw you down a whole ream of foolscap paper that you may fill all of it with the names of her beneficent institutions, the colleges and the asylums, the institutions of mercy, founded by infidelity, and supported by infidelity, pronounced against God; and the Christian religion and yet in favor of making the world better. "Oh," you say, "a ream of paper is too much for the names of those institutions." Well then, I throw you a quire of paper. Fill it it all up now. I will wait until you get all the names down. "Oh," you say, "that is too much." Well, then, I will just hand you a sheet of letter paper. Just fill up the four sides while we are talking of this matter. "Oh," you say, "that is too much room. We don't want a whole sheet of paper to write down the names." Perhaps I had better tear out one leaf from my hymn book, and ask you to fill up both sides of it with the names of such institutions. "Oh," you say, "that is too much room; you don't want so much room as that." Well then suppose you count them on your ten fingers. "Oh," you say, "not quite so much as that." Well, then, count them on the fingers of one hand. "Oh," you say, "not quite so many as that." Well, then, count on one finger the name of any institution founded by infidelity, supported by infidelity pronounced against God, and the Christian religion, yet toiling to make the world better. Not one! Not one! —TALMAGE.

INTEMPERANCE

"Nor drunkards shall inherit the Kingdom of God."—1 Cor. 6:10.

"No, I'll shun the hollow glee,
 And the mirth and revelry,
Where King Alcohol must be
 Crowned the monarch of the feast;
For this rosy-fingered devil,
 Prince and priest of all things evil,
While this poor weak head is level,
 Ne'er shall make a slave of me."

"DROWNING CARE"

Some men drink to excess to drown care. As well may a man in debt drink to drown his thoughts; it neither pays the debt, nor postpones the reckoning. O, soul, be true to thyself. When conscience is uneasy, it is foolish as well as wicked to attempt to smother its cries with worldly merriment—SPURGEON.

A DRUNKARD SAVED

Look you, down there in the dark alleys of New York is a poor drunkard. If you want to get near hell, go to a poor drunkard's home. Go to the house of that poor miserable drunkard. See the want and distress that reigns there. But hark! A footstep is heard at the door, and the children run and hide themselves. The patient wife waits to meet him. The man has been her torment. Many a time she has borne about for weeks the marks of blows. Many a time that strong right hand has been brought down on her defenceless head. And now she waits, expecting to hear his oaths, and to receive his brutal treatment.

He comes in and says to her: "I have been to the meeting, and I heard there, that if I will, I can be converted. I believe that God is able to save me." Go down to that house in a few weeks and see what a change! As you approach, you have some one singing. It is not the song of a reveller, but "The Bock of Ages." The children are no longer afraid of him, but cluster around his knee. His wife is near him, her face lit up with a happy glow. I can take you to thousands of homes made happy by such power of the religion of Christ. O ye slaves to drink, or sin of any kind, God will give you power to overcome temptation, and to lead a right life.—MOODY.

TWO CHILDREN

In the country I have often seen a little child, with her sun-browned face and long golden locks, sweet as any flower she pressed beneath her naked foot; merry as any bird that sung from bush or brake, driving the cattle home; and with fearless hand controlling the sulky leader of the herd, as with armed forehead and colossal strength he quailed before that slight image of God. Some days ago I saw a different sight—such a child, with hanging head, no music in his voice, nor blush but that of shame upon his cheek, leading home a drunken father upon the public street The man required to be led, guided, guarded. And into a condition hardly less helpless large masses of our people have sunk. Why do they drink? Look at their unhappy and most trying circumstances. Many of them are born with a propensity to this vice. They suck it in with a mother's milk. The drunken parent transmits to his children a proneness to his fatal indulgence. The foul atmosphere which many of them breathe, the hard labor by which many of them earn their bread, produce a prostration which seeks in stimulants something to rally the system, nor will they be debarred from their use by any prospect of danger. With our improved tastes, our books, our recreations, our domestic comforts, we have no adequate idea of the temptations to which the poor are exposed, and from which nothing is truer kindness than to protect them.—GUTHRIE.

INTEMPERANCE AMONG WOMEN

I am told that it is becoming more and more fashionable for women to drink; and it is not very long ago that a lady of great respectability, in this city, having taken two glasses of wine away from home, became violent, and her friends, ashamed, forsook her, and she was carried to a police station, and afterward to her disgraced home. I care not how well a woman may dress, if she has taken enough of wine to flush her cheek, and put a glassiness on her eye, she is intoxicated. She may be handed into a 2,500 dollar carriage, and have enough of diamonds to confound the Tiffanys—she is intoxicated. She may be a graduate of Packer Institute, and the daughter of some man in danger of being nominated for the Presidency, she is drunk. You may have a larger vocabulary than I have, and you may say in regard to her that she is "convivial," or she is "merry," or she is "festive," or she is "exhilarated"; but you can not with all your garlands of verbiage, cover up the fact that it is an old-fashioned case of drunk. —TALMAGE.

A WARNING

The victim pauses, gazes around upon the scene about his path of sin, and whispers, "Is it harmless?" "Harmless!" responds a serpent from the grass. Harmless! echo the sighing winds. Harmless! re-echo a hundred airy tongues. If now a gale from heaven might only sweep the clouds away through which the victim gazes! O, it God would break that potent power which chains the blasts of hell, and let the sulphur-stench roll up the vale, how would the vision change—the road become a track of dead men's bones, the heavens a lowering storm, the balmy breezes distant wailings, and all those balsam-shrubs that lied to his senses sweat drops of blood upon their poison boughs!

Ye who are meddling with the edges of vice, ye are on this road, and utterly duped by its enchantments. Your eye has already lost its honest glance, your taste has lost its purity, your heart throbs with poison. The leprosy is all over you; its blotches and eruptions cover you. Your feet stand on slippery places, whence in due time they shall slide, if you refuse the warning which I raise.— BEECHER.

JUDGMENT

"For we must all stand before the judgment seat of Christ."— 1 Cor. 5:10.

Before me place in dread array,
The pomp of that tremendous day,
   When thou with clouds shalt come
To judge the nations at thy bar;
And tell me, Lord, shalt I be there
   To meet a joyful doom?
      —CHARLES WESLEY.

The day of wrath, that dreadful day,
When heaven and earth shall pass away,
What power shall be the sinner's stay,
How shall he meet that dreadful day?
      —SIR WALTER SCOTT.

THE CROWNING DAY OF RECKONING

    The word of God teaches us plainly that there is future retribution; if it does not teach that it does not teach anything. If it tells us about the glory of heaven, and the mansions that Christ has gone to prepare, it tells us also about the torments of hell; it tells about the rich man lifting up his face in torment and crying for water. Now some people say, "Oh, you are just trying to scare us, you say such things just to alarm us." I would consider myself an unfaithful servant if I did not so warn you. The blood of your soul would be required at my hands if I did not so warn you Christ says, "How shall you escape the damnation of hell?" No one spoke of the judgment as Christ did; none knew it as well as he.—MOODY.

OUR RECORD

We shall meet again all we are doing and have done. The graves shall give up their dead, and from the tombs of oblivion the past shall give up all that it holds in keeping, to be witness for or witness against us. Oh, think of that, and in yonder hall of the inquisition see what its effect should be. Within those blood-stained walls, for whose atrocious cruelties Rome has yet to answer, one is under examination. He has been assured that nothing he reveals shall be written for the purpose of being used against him. While making frank and ingenious confession he suddenly stops. He is dumb—a mute. They ply him with questions, flatter him, threaten him; he answers not a word. Danger makes the senses quick. His ear has caught a sound; he listens; it ties his tongue. An arras hangs beside him, and behind it he hears a pen running along the pages. The truth flashes on him. Behind that screen a scribe sits committing to the fatal page every word he says, and he shall meet it again on the day of trial. Ah! how solemn to think that there is such a pen going in heaven, and entering on the books of judgment all we say, or wish, all we think or do.—GUTHRIE.

AN AWFUL FACT

A young woman, dying, said to her father! "Father, why did you not tell me there was a hell?" "Jennie, there is no such place. God is merciful. There will be no future suffering." She said: "I know better! I feel it now! I know there is such a place! My feet are slipping into it this moment I am lost! Why did you not tell me there was such a place?" It is the awful, stupendous, consuming, incontrovertible fact of the universe —TALMAGE.

HARSHNESS IN JUDGMENT

We ought to be induced away from all harshness by the fact that we ourselves are to be brought into high tribunal at the last, and that he shall have judgment without mercy that has shown no mercy. You are accustomed with rough grip to shake men for their misdeeds, waiting for no palliations, listening to no appeals. What will become of you, when at last, with all your imperfections, you stand before the bar of your Maker.—IBID.

THE SINNERS'S DOOM

To the Christian the shadow of death is the golden haze which heaven's light makes when it meets the earth. But to the sinner these shall be shadows full of phantom shapes. Images of terror in the future shall dimly rise and beckon thee, ghastly deeds of the past shall stretch out their skinny hands to push thee forward. Thou shalt not die unattended. Despair shall mock thee. Agony shall tender to thy parched lips her fiery cup. Remorse shall feel for thy heart, and rend it open. Good men shall breathe freer at thy death, and utter thanksgiving when thou art gone. Men shall place thy grave-stone as a monument and testimony that a plague is stayed, no tears shall wet it, no mourner linger there. And, as borne by the blast thy guilty spirit whistles toward the gate of hell; the hideous shrieks of those whom thy hand hath destroyed shall pierce thee—hell's first welcome.—BEECHER.

DAY OF SETTLEMENT FORGOTTEN

Is it not foolish to be living in this world without a thought of what you will do at last? A man goes into an inn, and as soon as he sits down he begins to order his wine, his dinner, his bed; there is no delicacy in season which he forgets to bespeak. He stops at the inn for some time. By and by the bill is forthcoming, and it takes him by surprise. "I never thought of that, I never thought of that!" "Why,'1 says the landlord, ' here is a man who is either a born fool or else a knave. What! never thought of the reckoning—never thought of settling with me!" After this fashion too many live, they eat and drink and sin, but they forget the inevitable hereafter, when for all the deeds done in the body, the Lord will bring us into judgment—SPURGEON.

LIFE

"What is your life."—James 4:14.

Life, I know not what thou art,
But know that thou and I must part;
And when or how or where we met,
I own to me's a secret yet.

Life, we've been long together,
Through pleasant and through cloudy weather
'Tis hard to part when friends are dear,—
Perhaps 'twill cost a sigh, a tear;
   —Then steal away, give little warning,
Choose thine own time;
Say not "Good night,"—but in some fairer clime
   Bid me "Good morning."
        —ANNA L. BARBAULD.

"ACT IN THE LIVING PRESENT"

What we do, we had better do right away. The clock ticks now and we hear it. After a while the clock will tick and we will not hear it. Seated by a country fireside, I saw the fire kindle, blaze, and go out. I gathered up from the hearth enough for profitable reflections. Our life is just like the fire on that hearth. We put on fresh fagots, and the fire bursts through and up and out, gay of flash, gay of crackle—emblem of boyhood. Then the fire reddens into coals; the heat is fiercer; and the more it is stirred the more it reddens. With sweep of flame it cleaves its way until all the hearth glows with the intensity—emblem of full manhood. Then comes a whiteness to the coals. The heat lessens. The flickering shadows have died along the wall. The fagots drop apart. The household hover over the expiring embers. The last breath of smoke has been lost in the chimney. The fire is out. Shovel up the white remains. Ashes!—TALMAGE.

LAUNCH OUT

The voyage of life should be right across the ocean, whose waters never shrink, and where the keel never rubs the bottom. But men are afraid to venture, and hang upon the coast, and explore lagoons, or swing at anchor in wind sheltered bays. Some men put their keel into riches, some into sensuous pleasures, some into friendship, and all these are shallow for anything that draws as deep as the human soul does. God's work in each age, indicated by the great movements of His providence, is the only thing deep enough for the heart. We ought to begin life as the source of a river, growing deeper every league to the sea; whereas, in fact thousands are like men who enter the mouths of rivers and sail upwards; finding less and less water every day; and in old age they lie shrunk and gaping upon dry gravel. —BEECHER.

WRECKS

Sailing down the Thames one occasionally sees a green flag in tatters, inscribed with the word WRECK, floating in the breeze over a piece of mast, or the funnel of a steamer which is just visible above the water. Alas! how many lifes might thus be marked, and how needful that they should be so labeled, lest they prove ruinous to others! The debauched, the self-rightoous, the spendthrift, the miserly, the apostate, the drunken; how wisely might the flag be placed over them, for they are WRECKS.—SPURGEON.

BURDEN-BEARING

Religious life is a life of burden-bearing. Fret not against your crosses, and they will be light. The yoke sits easiest on the neck of the patient ox. He feels his chain the lightest who does not drag but carry it. Bow before your trials, as I have read travelers do when overtaken in the desert by the dreadful Simoom. The Simoom! When that cry arises, striking terror into the boldest hearts, and the purple haze sweeps on, which to breath is death, they make no attempt to fly—the swiftest Arab scours not the desert like the wing of this scourge—but, instantly, they throw themselves on the ground, every head is muffled; and there, low in the dust, trembling, dumb, in awful silence they lie, and let the poisonous wind blow over them. "Hide thee in the dust, hide thee in the dust!" is the voice of God in our life calamities; and the lower we lie before Him, we shall suffer the less when darkness comes. —GUTHRIE.

WHAT IS MY LIFE?

My life. A ship that started well. All canvas set. A fair wind. A sea all sun. Then a cloud; then a lurid glare; then a lightning bolt, and the ship staggered in pain and fright. A great north wind, harsh, mighty, tempestuous, and then a sickening fear that I might never reach the shore. Perhaps go down in mid sea; perhaps perish in sight of land; perhaps go in more lost than found, a wreck to cry over.

My life? A bright bird, tuneful, brilliant, exceedingly; singing as I soar; cleaving the wind and getting higher and higher, and singing more blithely and more still; when an arrow strikes me, and I fall bleeding to the earth. Music gone; heart going; nothing but my own blood about me.

What is my life? A sullied robe; a crime concealed; a treason against God. I "know the right and yet the wrong pursue." I have sinned. I have grieved my Maker. I have played the mean trick; kept back the price; spoken the false word; said "yes," meant "no"; thought of self first, others last and least. The prayer has been upon my tongue, the loved sin under it. The hymn religious has not cleansed the mouth that sang it. I have bent my knee in prayer and straightened it again to fight. I have wept over sin, and done again that sin that made me weep. I have stopped half way home, and gone back to have one more day with the devil. I see oaths, vows, promises, lying behind me like tender blossoms shaken from the branches by rough winds in the spring time. My heart aches with the question "What shall I do?"

And the great answer is, "Do nothing of thyself." All is done for thee. The great Christ of God asks for no help of thine. One touch of his heart's blood and thou art born again; thou art a child, the universe is thine, the stars thy playthings, and the sky thy home.—PARKER.

LITTLE THINGS

"Who hath despisid the day of small things?"—Zach 4:10.

>   Let us be content to work,
> To do the thing we can, and not presume
> To fret because it's little. 'Twill employ
> Seven men, they say to make a perfect pin.
> Who makes the head consents to leave the point;
> Who makes the point agrees to miss the head;
> And if a man should cry, "I want a pin,
> And I must make it straightway head and point,"
> His wisdom is not worth the pin he wants.
>   —MRS. E. B. BROWNING.

LITTLE SINS AND BIG SINS

You will find many a merchant who, while he is so careful that he would not take a yard of cloth or a spool of cotton from the counter without paying for it, and who, if a bank cashier should make a mistake and send in a roll of bills five dollars too much would dispatch a messenger in hot haste to return the surplus, yet who will go into a stock company in which after a while he gets control of the stock, then waters the stock and makes $100,000 appear like $200,000. He only stole $100,000 by the operation. Many of the men of fortune made their wealth in that way. One of those men, engaged in such unrighteous acts, that evening, the evening of the very day when he watered the stock, will find a wharf-rat stealing a Brooklyn Eagle from the basement doorway, and will go out and catch the urchin by the collar, and twist the collar so tightly the fellow can't talk, but grip the collar tighter and tighter, saying, "I have been looking for you a long while; you stole my paper four or five times, didn't you? you miserable wretch." And then the old stock gambler, with a voice they can hear three blocks away, will cry out, "Police, police!" Prisons for sins insectile, but palaces for crimes dromedarian. No mercy for sins animalcule in proportion, but great leniency for mastodon iniquity. A poor boy slyly takes from the basket of a market woman a choke pear—saving some one else from the cholera—and you smother him in the horrible atmosphere of Raymond street jail, or New York Tombs, while his cousin, who has been skillful enough to steal $50,000 from the city, you will make a candidate for the New York Legislature.—TALMAGE.

DANGER OF LITTLE SINS

Be fearful of little sins. Take alarm at even an evil thought, wish, desire. These are the germs of sin—the floating seeds which drop into the heart, and finding in our natural corruption a fat and favorable soil, spring up into actual transgressions. These, like the rattle of the snake, the hiss of the serpent, reveal the presence and near neighborhood of danger. The experience of all good men proves that sin is most easily crushed in the bud, and that it is safer to flee from temptation than to fight it.—GUTHRIE.

POSSIBILITY OF LITTLE BEGINNINGS

When the air balloon was first invented, a matter of fact gentleman contemptuously asked Dr. Franklin what was the use of it. The doctor answered this question by asking another:—"What is the use of a new-born infant?" It may become a man. This anticipation of great things springing from small beginnings should induce us to put into practice those holy promptings which at certain seasons move our souls. What if we ourselves and our work should be little in Zion; cannot the Lord cause the grandest issues to proceed from insignificant beginnings?—SPURGEON.

THIS PRINCIPLE IN SOUL WINNING

Now all men that angle, or catch fish by the hook and line, know that it is individual work. It is one at a time. And when men so work, they are the servants of the fish. No man can walk out in lordly boots, and with admirable fixtures, gold and silver on his line, and say to the trout, "Here I am, come up here." No man can take what bait he chooses, and throw it in, and then with reason damn the fish because they do not bite.

In the preaching of the Gospel it is the business of every preacher to preach to every man and to all men. There is no great and there is no small before the coming of the sun. To the sun all things are small and all things are great, and they all alike receive beneficent power from it.—BEECHER.

SMALL DEFICIENCES OBSTACLES TO GRACE

There was only a hill between Israel and the land of promise. Surely the space being so small some concession will be made to Israel? If God could concede one inch to the bad man, he could concede all heaven. A ship may go down within ten feet of the shore; the vessel that has come proudly over the main may be wrecked in the channel. Heaven may be lost by an apparently insignificant deficiency. No action is to be regarded as of but secondary importance. We cannot regard our friend six days out of seven and disregard him on the seventh. Every moment of time is due to those with whom we have covenanted as to its duties and its remuneration.—PARKER.

LOVE

"Love is the fulfilling of the law."—Rom. 5:13.

"I say to thee, do thou repeat
To the first man thou mayest meet,
That he, and you, and all men more
Under a canopy of love,
Broad as the open sky above."

"Love? I will tell you what it is to love!
It is to build with human hearts a shrine,
Where hope sits brooding like a beauteous dove,
Where time seems young, and life a thing divine."
—CHARLES SWAIN.

LOVE LIKE A FLOWER SEED

Love, in this world, is like a seed taken from the tropics, and planted where the winter comes too soon; and it cannot spread itself in flower clusters, and wide twining vines, so that the whole air is filled with the perfume thereof. But there is to be another summer for it yet. Care for the root now, and God will care for the top by and by.— BEECHER.

NEED OF LOVE

Frequently at the great Roman games, the emperors, in order to gratify the citizens of Rome, would cause sweet perfumes to be rained down upon them through the awning which covered the amphitheatre. Behold the vases, the huge vessels of perfume! Yes, but there is naught here to delight you so long as the jars are sealed; but let the vases be opened, and be poured out, and let the drops of perfumed rain begin to descend, and every one is refreshed and gratified thereby. Such is the love of God. There is a richness and a fullness in it, but it is not perceived till the spirit of God pours it out like the rain of fragrance over the heads and hearts of all the living children of God. See, then, the need of having the love of God shed abroad in the heart by the Holy Ghost.—SPURGEON.

POWER OF LOVE

In Chicago a few years ago, there was a little boy who went to one of the mission Sunday-schools. His father moved to another part of the city about five miles away, and every Sunday that boy came past thirty or forty Sunday-schools to the one he attended. And one Sunday a lady who was out collecting scholars for a Sunday-school met him and asked him why he went so far, past so many schools. "There are plenty of others," said she, "just as good." "Ah," he said, "they may be just as good, but they are not so good for me." "Why not?" she asked. "Because they love a fellow over there," he answered. Ah! love won him. "Because they love a fellow over there!" How easy it is to reach people through love.— MOODY.

GIVE MY LOVE TO JESUS

The world owes its love to Jesus. Dear Jesus! Faithful Jesus! Loving Jesus! What fine Soar was in that day to Samaria, Jesus Christ is to all who take him. No wonder the little child, having been told that her playmate was dying, asked to be lifted up to see her. They lifted her up, and she kissed her dying playmate, and said, "Clara, give my love to Jesus.'" If Christ were fully known, the whole world would throw its arm around his neck.—TALMAGE.

SOUL-WINNING BY LOVE

A Christian woman went to the tract house in New York, and asked for tracts for distribution. The first day she was out on her Christian errand she saw a policeman taking an intoxicated woman to the station house. After the woman was discharged from custody, this Christian tract distributor saw her coming away all unkempt and unlovely. The tract distributor went up, threw her arms about her neck and kissed her. The woman said, "O my God, why do you kiss me?" "Well," replied the other, "I think Jesus told me to." "Oh no," the woman said, "don't you kiss me; it breaks my heart: nobody has kissed me since my mother died." But that loving, sisterly kiss brought her to Christ, started her on her way to heaven.—IBID.

LOVE STRONG AS DEATH

I look on this mother, who stands with her child on the side of the sinking wreck, to catch the last chance of a passing boat. She catches it—not to leap in herself; but, lifting her boy in her arms, and printing a mother's last kiss upon his rosy lips, she drops him, and remains behind herself to drown and die. Or I look at that maid in old border story, who, having caught a glance of the arrow that, shot by a rival's hand, came from the bushes on the other bank, flung herself before her lover, and received the fatal shot in her own true and faithful heart. I look at these things, and seeing that love is strong as death, I urge you to cultivate the love of Jesus, and go in its divine strength to the field of duty, and to the altar of sacrifice. —GUTHRIE.

MAN

"What is man, that Thou art mindful of him?"—Psa. 8:4.

>Man is a watch, wound up at first but never
>Wound up again: once down he's down forever.
>The watch once down, all motions then do cease;
>And man's pulse stopped, all passions sleep in peace.
>—ROBERT HERRICK.

DEMAND FOR GOOD MEN

In a hot summer's day some years ago, I was sailing with a friend in a tiny boat, on a miniature lake, enclosed like a cup within a circle of steep, bare Scottish hills. On the shoulder of the brown sun-burnt mountain, and full insight, was a well with a crystal stream trickling over its lip, and making its way down to the lake. Around the well's mouth and along the course of the rivulet, a belt of green stood out in strong contrast with the iron surface of the rocks all around. We soon agreed as to what should be made of it. There it was, a legend clearly printed by the finger of God on the side of these silent hills, teaching the passer-by how needful a good man is, and how useful he may be in a desert world.—SPURGEON.

THE BEST MONUMENT

What monument is appropriate for the grave of a godless man? What for the resting place of a Christian? It seems to me after I am dead and gone, I would rather have a man come to my grave and drop a tear, and say, "Here lies the man who converted me: who brought me to the cross of Christ"—it seems to me I had rather have this than a column of pure gold reaching to the skies, built in my honor. If a man wants to be useful, let him follow Christ.—MOODY.

THE WORTH OF MAN

If the value of anything is to be estimated by its price, to what an immeasurable height of worth does it exalt man that God gave His Son to redeem him!—redeeming him not with corruptible things such as silver and gold, but with the precious blood of Christ; as of a lamb without spot or blemish. So far from cherishing low views of man, I believe that a gem of inestimable value lies concealed beneath the beggar's rags. A soul is there of divine-like faculties and of priceless worth: and a body also, which, though the seat of appetites that man shares with brutes, and of passions, perhaps, such as burn in the breast of fiends, may become more sacred than any fane built by human hands—a temple of the Holy Ghost. There is a worth in man no meanness of circumstances, no degradation of character can altogether conceal. He is a jewel, though buried in a heap of corruption; the vilest outcast, possessing powers and affections that need only to be sanctified to ally him with angels, and make publicans and harlots fit for Heaven.—GUTHRIE.

MAN'S EXALTED NATURE

I look at man's moral nature. Made in the image of God. Vast capacity for enjoyment, capable at first of eternal joy and, though now disordered, still through the recuperative grace of God, able to mount up to more than its original felicity: faculties that may blossom and bear fruit inexhaustibly. Immortality written on every capacity: a soul destined to range in unlimited spheres of activity long after the world has put on ashes, and the solar system shall have snapped its axle, and the stars that, in their courses, fought against Sisera, shall have been slain, and buried amid the tolling thunders of the last day.—TALMAGE.

A NAME OF POWER

It makes no difference what you call men—prince, peer, or slave. Man is that name of power which rises above them all, and gives to every one the right to be that which God meant he should be. No law nor custom, nor opinion, nor prejudice has the right to say to one man, "You may grow," and to another, "You may not grow," or, "You may grow in ten directions, and not in twenty;" or to the strong, "You may grow stronger," or to the weak, "You may never become strong." Launched upon the ocean of life, like an innumerable fleet, each man may spread what sails God has given him, whether he be pinnace, sloop, brig, bark, ship, or man of war; and no commodore or admiral may signal what voyage he shall make or what canvas he shall carry.—BEECHER.

THE PRIMEVAL MAN

"God made man in His image." There is surely no bolder sentence in all human speech. It takes an infinite liberty with God! It is blasphemy if it is not truth. We have been accustomed to look at the statement so much from the human standpoint, that we have forgotten how deeply the Divine character is implicated. To tell us that all the sign-boards of Italy were painted by Raphael is simply to dishonor and bitterly humiliate the great artist. We would resent the suggestion that Beethoven or Handel is the author of all the noise that goes under the name of music. Yet we say God made man. Look at man, and then repeat the audacity if you dare! Lying, drunken, selfish man; plotting, scheming, cruel man; foolish, vain, babbling man; prodigal man, wandering in wildernesses in search of the impossible, sneaking in forbidden places with the crouch of a criminal, putting his finger into human blood and musing as to its probable price per gallon—did God make man? Verily then, a strange image is God's! Leering, gibing, mocking image; a painted mask; a vigor meant to deceive. See where cunning works in its own well-managed wrinkle—see how cold selfishness puts out the genial warmth of eyes that should have beamed with kindness; hear how mean motives have taken the music out of voices that should have expressed more truthful frankness; then look at the body, misshapen, defiled, degraded, rheum in every joint, specks of corruption in the warm currents of the blood, leprosy making the skin loathsome, the whole body tottering under the burden of the invisible, but inseparable companionship of death! Is this the image, is this the likeness of God? Or take man at his best estate—what is he but a temporary success in art, clothier's art, schoolmaster's art, fashion's art? He cannot see into to-morrow; he imperfectly remembers what happened yesterday; he is crammed for the occasion, made great for the little battle, careful about the night air, dainty as to his digestion, sensitive to praise or blame, preaching gospels and living blasphemies, praying with forced words, whilst his truant mind is uneasy in the thick of markets, or the complicity of contending interests. Is this the image of God? Is this incarnate Deity? Oh, how we burn under the sharp questioning! Yet there are the facts. There are the men themselves. Write on the low brow— "the image and likeness of God;" write on the idiot's leering face—"the image and likeness of God;" write on the sensualist's porcine face—the image and likeness of God;" do this; and then say how infinite is the mockery, how infinite the lie! Yet here is the text Here is the distinct assurance that God created man in His own image. This is enough to ruin the Bible. This is enough to dethrone, God. Within narrow limits any man would be justified in saying, "If man is made in the image of God, I will not worship a God who bears such an image."

What is to be done? We are driven back upon our-selves—not ourselves as outwardly seen, but our inner selves, the secret of our soul's reality.

Aye; we are now nearing the point We have not been talking about the right man at all. The man is within the man; the man is not any one man; the man is Humanity. We have never seen the true man; he has been seen only by his Maker. As to temper and action, we are all bankrupts and criminals. But the man is greater than the sin. When I see the sinner run into sin, I feel as if he might have been made by the devil, but when he stands still and bethinks himself; when the hot tears fill his eyes; when he sighs toward heaven a sigh of bitterness and true penitence, when he falls down to pray without words; then I see a dim outline of the image and likeness in which he was created. In that solemn hour I begin to see man—the man that accounts for the Cross, the man who brought down Christ. —PARKER.

MARRIAGE

"Marriage is honorable in all."—Heb. 13:4. "What therefore God has joined together, let no man put asunder."—Matt. 19:4.

> Grabbed age and youth
>   Cannot live together;
> Youth is full of pleasance
>   Age is full of care;
> Youth like summer mom,
>   Age like winter weather;
> Youth like summer brave,
>   Age like winter bare,
> Youth is full of sport,
>   Age's breath is short.
>   —SHAKESPEARE.

> Marriage is the golden chain
>   That binds two hearts together
> For pleasure or for pain.
>   For storm or pleasant weather.
>   —CHAS. BENJ. MANLY.

JOY AT A WEDDING

If the hard brow ever relaxes, it is at a wedding. The nature cold and unsympathetic thaws out under the glow, and the tears start as we hear the bride's dress rustling down the stairs and the company stands back, and we hear in the timid "I will" of the twain, the sound of a lifetime's hopes and joys and sorrows. We look steadily at them, but thrice at her to once at him, and say, "God bless her, how well she looks!" We cry at weddings, but not bitter tears; for when the heart is stirred, and smiles are insipid, and the laughter is tame, the heart writes out its joy on the cheek in letters of crystal. Put on the ring! Let it ever be bright, and the round finger it encloses never be shrunken with sorrow.—TALMAGE.

UNHAPPY MARRIAGES

Marriages are said to be made in heaven. No, oh no! There may be a world of difference between the two who are joined together; and marriage is a sphere for heroism on that very account. What tragedies! What wondrous lives! The story of Daniel in the lion's den, and of the four in the burning furnace, are typical of the angelic virtues that are found in women that walk in the very midst of hell for years and lives. I cannot conceive of any life so horrible as that of a pure, high-minded woman, a virtuous and aspiring soul, allied to trickery, to lying, to all lecherous vices, to drunkenness and the worst forms of animalism. To sleep with swine, to nestle with serpents, to be with loathsome insects that gnaw and sting, is bad enough; but to be with them altogether in the shape of a man is hideous beyond conception. Dante, in his vision, never saw anything worse than that which exists in some married lives.—BEECHER.

"UNEQUALLY YOKED TOGETHER"

I do not believe a Christian man has a right to marry any unconverted woman. I do not believe any Christian woman has a right to marry an unconverted man. I imagine you will laugh about it and ridicule the whole idea, but here is the word of God for it. "Be ye not unequally yoked together with unbelievers." "Wherefore come out from among them and be ye separate." Now I never knew any one to go against the Bible that did not suffer for it. Let him that takes off the harness laugh, not him that puts it on. It is not for you, young people, that have not seen as much of life and the world as some others, to say that you can go right on and dispute this thing. You can see it is plain. There is not a mother here that would not feel badly to have her daughter marry a man that could not bear her, but would only make her wretched and abuse her. There is no father here who would not be made miserable by such a possibility. Do you suppose that God does not feel it to have His sons and daughters marry unregenerate and unconverted persons who hate Him, doubt Him, and misrepresent Him.— MOODY.

A TENDER TIE

In looking back to the first marriage, I cannot but think that it was to make its tie more tender that God chose the singular plan he pursued in providing the man with a mate. No other way would have occurred to our fancy of making woman, than that of another clay figure, modeled by God's hands in the female form, and inspired by His breath with life. In making her out of Adam, and from the part of his body lying nearest the heart, while he lay in the mysterious sleep from which he awoke to gaze on a beautiful form reposing by his side, God gave a peculiar emphasis and power to the figure, "they twain shall be one flesh," one in sympathy, in mind, in affections, and in interests; nothing but death afterward to divide them.—GUTHRIE.

MISSIONS

"Go ye into all the world, and preach the gospel to every creature."—Mark 16:15.

> Where is your heathen brother? From his grave
>   Near thy own gates, or 'neath a foreign sky,
> From the thronged depths of ocean's mourning wave,
>   His answering blood reproachfully doth cry:
> Blood of the soul! Can all earth's fountains make
> Thy dark stain disappear? Stewards of God, awake.
>   —MRS. SIGOURNEY.

OUR FIELD, THE WORLD

The mission spirit has now gained such momentum and rapidity, that we can now go through a revolution, changing public sentiment from selfishness to benevolence, in twenty-five or thirty years. We know that the influence of Calvary can never die. I may die in the wilderness, and you may die on the sea; but the road to heaven is as short from India as it is from Indiana, and when once in heaven we shall see a much better sight than Moses saw from the top of Pisgah, and everyone may gaze on it who has done one jot or one tittle to advance the work. Whisper it then into the ears of your children, that "the field is the world!" Ye who are bringing up your own flesh and blood to delight in dress, in worldly aggrandizement, in wealth, in ambition, in honor, have you not seen what the Lord is doing? Have you not seen that his service is becoming the path to honor? That working for the world is the shortest road to promotion in our day? Teach your children to give up their soul and body and strength to their Master's service. Thus shall they be nearer to God, and God to them. We must not live for ourselves, but for others.—BEECHER.

AN EARNEST FLEA

If there were but one man in Siberia unsaved, and all the world were saved besides, if God should move our minds, it would be worthwhile for all the people in England to go after that one soul. Did you ever think of the value of a soul? Ah! ye have not heard the howls and yells of hell; ye have not heard the mighty songs and hosannas of the glorified; ye have no notion of what eternity is, or else ye would know the value of a soul.

Permit me, with all earnestness, to plead with you, on behalf of Christ, and Christ's holy gospel, that you would stir yourselves up to renewed efforts for the spread of His truth, and to more earnest prayers that His kingdom may come. Ah! could I show you the tens of thousands of spirits who are now walking in outer darkness; could I take you to the gloomy chamber of hell, and show you myriads upon myriads of souls in unutterable torture, me-thinks you could ask yourselves: "Did I do anything to save these unhappy myriads?" They have been damned, and are you clear of their blood? "If the watchman warn them not, they shall perish, but their blood will He require at the watchman's hands."—SPURGEON.

"UNTO EVERY CREATURE"

I can imagine Peter saying, "Lord, do you really mean that we shall preach the gospel to every creature?" "Yes, Peter." "Shall we go back to Jerusalem and preach the gospel to those sinners who murdered you?" "Yes, Peter, go back and tarry there until you are endued with power from on high. Offer the gospel to them first. Go search out that man who spat in my face; tell him I forgive him; there is nothing in my heart but love for him. Go, search out that man who put the cruel crown of thorns on my brow; tell him I will have a crown ready for him in my kingdom, if he will accept salvation; there shall not be a thorn in it, and he shall wear it forever and ever in the kingdom of heaven. Find out that man who took the reed from my hand, and smote my head, driving the thorns deeper into my brow. If he will accept salvation as a gift, I will give him a sceptre, and he shall sway it as a king. Go, seek out that man who struck me with the palm of his hand; find him, and preach the gospel to him; tell him that the blood of Jesus Christ was shed for all men, and even for him, if he accepts it." Yes, I can imagine him saying, "Go, seek out that poor soldier who drove the spear into my side; tell him that there is a nearer way to my heart than that. Tell him that I forgive him freely; and tell him that I will make him a soldier of the cross, and my banner over him shall be love."

I thank God that the gospel is to be preached to every creature. Rich and poor, great and small, king and peasant, alike are welcome.—MOODY.

UNIVERSAL FRATERNITY

I am bound to preach the gospel to every creature, for all men are my brothers. The ignorant black man is my brother. His skin, to be sure, may have a different hue from mine; bred for the market, he may be bought and sold like a cattle-beast; he may be marked with the brand, loaded with the fetters, lashed with the whip, crushed with the sufferings of a slave; but he is my brother, and if he lift his manacled hands and streaming eyes to that heaven where bondsmen are free, and, robed and throned, they stand before Him, and share in the glory of His Son, slave though he be, sold though he be, trodden in the dust though he be, he may be my awed brother. With the same God for our Father, the same Savior for our Elder Brother, the same Spirit for our heavenly Comforter, one cross for the anchor of our hope, one Bible for our guidebook, one heaven for our everlasting home, the gospel tells me to knock off my brother's fetters—to loose them, and let them free.—GUTHRIE.

THE MISSIONARY OUTLOOK

Why, the earth is like an old castle with twenty gates and a park of artillery ready to thunder down every gate. Lay aside all Christendom, and see how all heathendom is being surrounded and honey-combed and attacked by this all-conquering gospel. At the beginning of this century there were only 150 missionaries; now there are 25,000 missionaries and native helpers and evangelists. At the beginning of this century there were only 50,000 heathen converts; now there are 1,650,000 converts from heathendom. There is not a sea-coast on the planet but the battery of the gospel is planted, and ready to march on, north, south, east, west. You all know that the chief work of an army is to plant the batteries, and they may do all the work in ten minutes. These batteries are being planted in all nations. It may take a good while to plant them, but they may do all their work in a little while. They will. Nations are to be born in a day. Hosts of the living God, march on, march on! The sky is brightening in every direction. I am glad for the boy and girl five years old: I think they may see the millennium. All nations will yet salute the flag of Prince Immanuel. To Him be glory in the church, throughout all ages.—TALMAGE.

MOTHER

"As one whom his mother comforteth."—Isaiah 66:13.

Such beautiful, beautiful hands,
    They're neither white nor small,
And you, I know, would scarcely think
    That they were fair at all.
I've looked on hands whose form and hue.
    A sculptor's dream might be,
Yet are my mother's wrinkled hands
    More beautiful to me.

And oh, beyond this shadow land,
    Where all is bright and fair,
I know full well those dear old hands
    Shall palms of victory bear.
Where crystal streams through endless years
    Flow over golden sands,
There, where the old grow young again,
    I'll clasp my mother's hands.

A SACRED NAME

More and more as we grow, we appreciate the finer traits of human nature. Men going out into life never forget the mother who stays at home, and who has presented to them a nature with reason dominant, with a high moral sense, with refined and sweet affections, with taste, with patience, with gentleness, with self-sacrifice, and with disinterestedness. A man may go through all the world; he may become a pirate, if you please; he may run through every stage of belief and unbelief; he may become absolutely apostate; he may rub out his conscience; he may destroy his fineness in every respect; but there will be one picture which he cannot efface. Living or dying there will rise before him, like a morning star, the beauty of that remembered goodness which he called mother.

There are men who are so cynical that they swear the whole race to hell; but they always spare some one person— wife, or sister, or mother. There is a single character that survives annihilation in their thoughts. There is nothing that takes hold of a man's very being so much as a nature that seems to be well nigh perfect.—BEECHER.

A SUGGESTIVE NAME

When one speaks the name of my mother, and says to me, "Roxana," it is no Greek that I think of; it is she that was a Connecticut woman, bred in an obscure neighborhood, quiet and retiring, but full of deep pondering of things beyond her age, and of a heart rich and rare. And is there a person who has not a name—somebody's name— which, when he hears it, distils a sweet influence upon his imagination, or rains down joyful emotive feelings on his heart? Names? They are wonder-workers. A single name will send fire through twenty thousand men. A name? When the united armies of the North returned from the sad but necessary war with the South, and marched through Washington, and Sherman's name was sounded in their ear, what a heaven-rending shout went up I Just one word was uttered, but what an effect it produced!—IBID.

MOTHER'S COMFORT

An aged mother is almost omnipotent in comfort. Why? At seventy years of age she has been through it all. At seven o'clock in the morning she goes over to comfort a young mother who has just lost her babe. Grandmother knows all about that trouble. Fifty years ago she felt it. At twelve o'clock of that day she goes over to comfort a widowed soul. She knows all about that. She has been walking in that valley of shadow twenty years. At four o'clock in the afternoon some one knocks at the door wanting bread, She knows all about that. Two or three times in her life she came to her last loaf. At ten o'clock that night she goes over to sit up with some one who is severely sick. She knows all about it. She knows all about fevers, and pleurisies, and broken bones. She has been doctoring all her life, spreading plasters, and pouring out bitter drops, and shaking up hot pillows and contriving things to tempt a poor appetite. Doctors Abernethy, Rush, Hosack and Harvey were great doctors, but the greatest doctor the world ever saw was a Christian mother. Dear me I Do we not remember her about the room, when we were sick in our boyhood? Was there any one who could so touch a sore without hurting it? And when she lifted her spectacles against her wrinkled forehead, so she could look closer at the wound, it was three-fourths healed. And when the Lord took her home, although you may have been men and women thirty, forty, fifty years of age, you lay on the coffin-lid and sobbed as though you were only five or ten years of age. O man, praise God, if, instead of looking back to one of those berouged and bespangled old people, fixed up of the devil to look young, you have in your memory the picture of an honest, sympathetic, kind, self-sacrificing, Christ-like mother.—TALMAGE.

MOTHER'S FORGIVENESS

An Englishman told me a story once which may serve to illustrate how God forgives. There was a boy a good many years ago, stolen in London, the same as Charley Ross was stolen here. Long months and years passed away, and the mother prayed and prayed as that mother of Charley Boss has prayed, I suppose, and all her efforts had failed, and they had given up all hope; but the mother did not quite give up all her hope. One day a boy was sent up into the neighboring house to sweep the chimney, and by some mistake he got down through the wrong chimney. He came down through the sitting room chimney of that house. His memory began at once to travel back through the years that had passed. He thought that things looked strangely familiar. The scenes of his early childhood were dawning upon him; and as he stood there surveying the place, his mother came into the room. He stood there covered with rags and soot. Did she wait till she had sent him to be washed before she took him in her arms? No, indeed; it was her own boy. She took him to her arms, all black and smoke, and hugged him to her bosom, and shed tears of grateful joy upon his head. Such is God's love for the sinner, He will forgive, and receive him to Himself.

OLD AGE

"When I am old and grey-headed, O God, forsake me not."— Psa. 72:18.

Eye hath not seen, tongue hath not told,
    And ear hath not heard it sung,
How buoyant and bold,
Though it seem to grow old,
    Is the heart, forever young;.
Forever young—though life's old age
    Hath every nerve unstrung;
The heart, the heart is a heritage
    That keeps the old man young.
        —M. F. TUPPER.

VICE IN OLD AGE

According to Aesop, an old woman found an empty jar which had lately been full of prime old wine, and which still retained the fragrant smell of its former contents. She greedily placed it several times to her nose, and drawing it backwards and forwards said, "Oh, most delicious! How nice must the wine itself have been, when it leaves behind in the very vessel which contained it so sweet a perfume."

Men often hug their vices when their power to enjoy them is gone. The memories of reveling and wantonness appear to be sweet to the ungodly in their old age. They sniff the empty bottles of their follies, and only wish they could again be drunken with them. Old age cures not the evil heart, but exhibits in a ridiculous but deeply painful light the indelible perversity of human nature.—SPURGEON.

GROWING OLD UNCONSCIOUSLY

Old age comes on almost imperceptibly though the young, perhaps will hardly credit it. Men with furrows in their brow, and gray hairs on their head, often find it difficult to remember that they are old; to believe it, to realize the approach of their end; how near they are to the grave. Death seems to flee before us like the horizon which we ever see, and never reach. The river that springs like an arrow from its rocky cradle, to bound from crag to crag, to rush brawling through the glen, and, like thoughtless youth, to waste its strength in mere noise, and froth and foam, flows on smoothly, slowly, almost imperceptibly as it approaches its grave in the bosom of the sea. And so it is often with man. The nearer we draw to our end, through a natural callousness or otherwise, the less sensible we grow to the evils and approach of age. And when a man has not left his peace with God to seek in old age, his greatest work to a time when he is least fit to do it, it is a most blessed thing that old age does not make our hearts old, or benumb our feelings—that gray hairs are on us, and we know it not—GUTHRIE.

SAD OLD AGE

It is dismal to get old, without the rejuvenating influence of religion. When we step on the down grade of life, and see that it dips in the verge of the cold river, we want to behold some one near who will help us across. When the sight loses its power, we need that faith that can illumine. When we feel the failure of the ear, we need the dear tones of the divine voice. When the axe-men of death hew down whole forests of strength and beauty around us, and we are left in solitude, we need the dove to sing in our branches.—TALMAGE.

REJOICING IN OLD AGE

Look at old age! A friend said to me, a lady, "I hate old age," and there was a vehemency in it that left me no doubt as to the sincerity of the expression. A young friend wrote to me, "I can't bear to think that I am growing old." Such have no horizon. They have no foresight, I am growing old. Do I not know it? Do I not rejoice in it? I have had my life; I have had my opportunities; and I thank God for such as it has been. I thank God that my eye grows dim. I thank God that my steps are not so alert as once they were. Why should men mourn that beauty which must fade before the glorious beauty of holiness settles upon them forever.

When I see in the spring the trees full of bud, and ready to bloom in the orchard, I hear complaint from the outside green coating of the bud, that has wrapped it up like an overcoat, and has carried it through the winter. As the balmy atmosphere begins to expand the bud, I hear the sepal mourn and say: "Alas, alas! I am being expelled and pushed down, the hinges are breaking off; I have got to drop." And go it does in some high wind; but it goes in order that the blossom may live. Then after a little while, I hear the blossom say, "I must fall;" and fall it does to the ground, in order that the fruit may spring forth. Now, when men mourn because they are losing this faculty, and that faculty, they forget that they are failing here, in order that glorious virtues and perfect holiness may emerge to ripen forever in heaven.— BEECHER.

PATIENCE

"In your patience possess ye your souls."—Luke 21:19.

Be patient, oh, be patient! put your ear against the earth,
And listen there how noiselessly the germ of the seed has birth;
How noiselessly and gently it upheaves its little way,
Till it parts the scarcely broken ground and the blade stands up in day.

Be patient, oh, be patient! the germs of mighty thought
Must have their silent undergrowth, must underground be wrought;
But as sure as there's a power that makes the grass appear,
Our land shall be green with freedom, the blade-time shall be here.

IMPATIENCE REBUKED

I remember a few years ago I got discouraged and could not see much fruit of my work; and one morning, as I was in my study, cast down, one of my Sabbath-school teachers came in and wanted to know what I was discouraged about, and I told him, because I could see no result from my work; and, by and by, speaking about Noah, he said: "By the way, did you ever study up the character of Noah?" I felt that I knew all about that, and told him that I was familiar with it, and he said, "Now, if you never studied that carefully, you ought to do it, for I cannot tell you what a blessing it has been to me." When he went out I took down my Bible, and began to read about Noah, and the thought came stealing over me, "Here is a man who toiled and worked a hundred years and didn't get discouraged; or if he did, the Holy Ghost didn't put it on record; and the clouds lifted, and I got up and said, "If the Lord wants me to work without any fruit, I will work on. I will do the best I can and leave the result with God. I will wait patiently upon the Lord."—MOODY.

A PATIENT GOD

Our God is a God of patience—patience long continued but not everlasting. Swift fly the wings of mercy, slow goes the hand of justice; like the shadow on the sun-dial, ever moving, yet creeping slowly on, with a motion all but imperceptible. Still let sinners stand in awe. The hand of justice has not stopped, although imperceptibly, it steadily advances, by and by having reached the tenth, eleventh, twelfth hour, the bell strikes. Then, unless you soon flee to Christ, the blow which was so slow to fall shall descend on the head of impenitence with accumulated force. Let it never be forgotten, that although God's patience is lasting, it is not everlasting.—GUTHRIE.

MORE PATIENCE

What we all need is patience. Before we start off for the store we ought to pray for patience. We will be harassed and perplexed. Men will wrong us, and impose upon us, and cheat us; and before the day is passed, if you have not laid in a large supply of patience, you will half swear with your lips, and perhaps make a whole swear with your hearts.—TALMAGE.

THE TEACHING OF THE LEAVES

O impatient ones! Did the leaves say nothing to you as they murmured, when you came hither to-day? They were not created this spring, but months ago; and the summer just begun will fashion others for another year. At the bottom of every leaf stem is a cradle, and in it is an infant germ; and the winds will rock it, and the birds will sing to it all summer long, and next season it will unfold. So God is working for you, and carrying forward to the perfect development all the processes of your lives.— BEECHER.

PATIENCE IN SMALL EFFORTS

A poor woman had a supply of coal laid at her door by a charitable neighbor. A very little girl came out with a small fire shovel, and began to take up a shovelful at a time and carry it in. I said to the child, "Do you expect to get all that coal in with that little shovel?" She was confused at my question, but her answer was striking, "Yes, sir, if 1 work long enough." Humble worker, make up for your want of ability by abundant continuance in well-doing, and your life work will not not be trivial. Patience in small efforts will effect more than the occasional use of great talents.—SPURGEON

PATIENCE IN RETREAT

Patience is hard, sometimes. Whilst I am climbing the mountains, passing through the wilderness, daring dangers, I feel comparatively quiet, or even glad. But to sit down when the angel tells me to sit, and not to stir till he comes back again—who can do it?

There are lines of retreat in every great life, when Christ must be driven into Egypt, when the prophet must be banished into solitude, when John the Baptist must be in the desert eating locusts and wild honey, when Saul of Tarsus must be driven off into Arabia—times when "in patience we must possess our souls." But an asylum need not be a tomb, retreat need not be extinction. Make the best of your leisure. You want to be at the front, instead of that you have been banished to the rear. It is for a wise purpose. Gather strength, let the brain sleep, yield yourself to the spirit of the quietness of God, and after what appears to be wasted time or unprofitable waiting, there shall come an inspiration into thy soul that shall make thee strong and fearless, and the banished one shall become the center of nations.—PARKER.

POOR

"For ye have the poor always with you."—Matt. 26:11.

Think yon, indeed, Fate is unkind,
In poverty's dull chains to bind
Or fetter my aspiring mind?
    Ah! think again:
Lady, my Father is a King;
Around His Throne immortals sing,
    Their faces veil!
This beauteous world, this air-hung ball,
Sun, moon, and stars, both great and
My Father made, and owns them all;
    I am not poor.

NEAR THE SKIES

When men go up in balloons they take with them bags of sand for ballast, and when they want to rise higher they throw out some of the sand. Now there are some Christians who, before they rise higher, will have to throw out some ballast. If you have got overloaded, just throw out a little money, and you will mount up as on eagle's wings. The poor are often wealthier than the rich. They live nearer the skies, nearer to God.—MOODY.

PLEA FOR KINDNESS TO THE POOR

Let a man invite the poor to dinner, and how people would stop, and stare, and gaze with wonder at the stream of poverty creeping along and pouring in at his open door—the lame hobbling on crutches, the blind led by a dog, or little child, the widow clad in rusty weeds, the poor outcast with rags on her back and at her bosom a shrivelled infant, children shivering and shoeless, from streets their haunt by day, from dirty dens and cellars their cold home by night! Not wondered at only, and supposed by many to be mad, the man who dare do this, who would render a literal obedience to Christ's command, might prepare for no measured censure— people saying, this was to turn the world upside down; to spoil the poor; to inflate them with notions unbefitting their condition; to destroy the lines of demarcation which God in His providence had drawn between the different classes of society. What a talk such a feast would make! Nevertheless, why should it not be tried?—GUTHRIE.

MERCY FOR THE POOR

Thank God there is mercy for the poor! The great Dr. Mason preached over a hundred times the same sermon, and the text was, "To the poor the gospel is preached." Lazarus went up, while Dives went down; and there are candidates for imperial splendor in the back alleys and by the peat fire of the Irish shanty. King Jesus set up His throne in a manger and made a resurrection day for the poor widow of Nain, and sprang the gate of heaven wide open, so that all the beggars and thieves and scoundrels of the universe may come in if they only repent.—TALMAGE.

POVERTY AND HAPPINESS

It sometimes happens that poverty brings to a man what all his wealth had failed to give—happiness. A man too rich to be industrious is a prey to the thousand frets of unoccupied leisure. The want of proper occupation is the cause of more than half of the petty frets of life.

In this world, it is not what we take up, but what we give up, that makes us rich.

No man can tell by turning to his ledger whether he is rich or poor. It is the heart that makes a man rich. He is rich or poor, according to what he is, not according to what he has.—BEECHER.

DANGER OF GREAT RICHES

Crossing the Col D'Obbia, the mule laden with our luggage sank in the snow, nor could it be recovered until its load was removed, then, but not till then, it scrambled out of the hole it had made, and pursued its journey. This circumstance made us meditate upon the wise way in which the gracious

Father unloads us by our own losses, and brings us into the experience of poverty, that we may be able to pursue our journey to heaven, and not sink in the snow of carnal-mindedness.—SPURGEON.

THE POOR IN HEAVEN

In Christ's conception of the blessed life, I find mentioned many persons that I did not expect to find referred to, and I find many persons omitted that I expected would have been first referred to. Let me take the beatitudes as a picture of Heaven. Who is in Heaven? Blessed are the mighty, for they are in Heaven; blessed are the rich, for theirs is the kingdom of glory; blessed are the famous, for theirs are the trumpets of eternity; blessed are the noble, for the angels are their servants. Why, that is not the text. Who is in Heaven? The poor in spirit. Then, perhaps, we may be there. Not many mighty, not many noble, not many learned, not many brilliant are called; then perhaps we may be there. Woman, mother, sisters, obscure person, unknown life—you may be there.—PARKER.

POWER

"Tarry ye in the city of Jerusalem until ye be endowed with power from on high."—Luke 24:49.

Let our prayers to heaven ascending,
Earnest patient, never ending,
Cleave the air of earth and sky,
Reach the ear of Him on high,
For the gift of holy power,
For the vitalizing shower
Of the blessed spirit's presence
Every moment, every hour.
—CHAS. BENJ. MANLY.

To the hills we lift our vision,
   From whence must come all power,
And we pray to God the Father,
   To send like a gentle shower,
The spirit of light, of truth and might,
   To brighten our hearts and show us the way,
From the realms of night
   To unending day.
—IBID.

POWERLESS AND USELESS

Of what use would be the machinery which is to be moved, without a force adequate to move it? Without a main-spring within the clock, however complete all its wheels, pinions, pivots, and axles, these hands would stand on the face of time, nor advance one step over the numbered hours. So were it without the power of the spirit, with the renewed soul, to set its forces in action, bring them into play, and impart to them a true and heavenward character.—GUTHRIE.

POWER OF DEEP PIETY

A man of deep religious experiences is always effective. I care not how poor his voice is, or how uncomely his countenance, or how awkward his gestures, or how shabby his clothes, or how lame his grammar. By taking care of our own vineyard, we learn how to help others in the care of their vineyard.—TALMAGE.

THE TEST OF GODLINESS

The test of Godliness is power. The man who is like God in holiness, in love, in goodness, will have some of God's power. He will be a sun, around which, like celestial bodies around their solar center, smaller characters will revolve. His life will be forceful, magnetic, and crowded with results. His influence will be resistless, for men will look at him and say,—"He is a good man." He is, for God is in him.—BEECHER.

GETTING NEARER GOD

In driving piles, a machine is used by which a high weight is lifted up and then made to fall upon the head of the pile. Of course the higher the weight is lifted, the more powerful is the blow it gives when it descends. Now if we would tell upon our age, and tell upon society with ponderous blows, we must see to it that we are uplifted as near to God as possible. All our power will depend upon the elevation of our spirits. Prayer, meditation, communion, devotion, are like a windlass to wind us up aloft; it is not lost time which we spend in such sacred exercises, for we are thus accumulating force, so that when we come down to our actual religion—labor for God, we shall descend with an energy unknown to those to whom communion is unknown.—SPURGEON.

ANOINTING WITH POWER

I have in my mind a minister who said, "I have heart disease, I can't preach more than once a week," so he had a colleague to preach for him once a week and do the visiting. He was an old minister and couldn't do any visiting. He had heard of the anointing of power, and he said, "I would like to be anointed for my burial. I would like before I go hence to preach the gospel once with power He prayed that God would fill him with the spirit, and I met him not long after that, and he said, "I have preached on an average eight times a week, and I have had conversions all along." The spirit came on him. I don't believe that man broke down at first with hard work, so much as with using the machinery without oil, without lubrication. It is not the hard work which breaks down ministers, but it is the toil of working without power. Oh, that God may anoint His people! Not the ministry only, but every disciple.—MOODY.

PRAYER

"Men ought always to pray."—Luke 18:1.

I often say my prayers;
    But do I ever pray?
And do the wishes of my heart
    Go with the words I say?
I may as well kneel down,
    And worship gods of stone,
As offer to the living God
    A prayer of words alone,
For words without the heart
    The Lord will never hear;
Nor will He to those lips attend
    Whose prayers are not sincere.
        —JOHN BURTON

CONSISTENCY IN PRAYER

It is an outrage to ask God to do a thing while we sit indolent. The prayer to be acceptable, must come not only from the heart, but from the hands. Luther came to Melancthon's bedside and prayed for his recovery, and insisted, at the same time, that he should take some warm soup, the soup being just as important as the prayer.

If a man has "evening prayers" asking for health, and then sits down to a full supper of indigestibles at eleven o'clock at night, his prayer is a mockery. A man has no right to pray for the safety of his family when he knows there is no cover on the cistern.—TALMAGE.

THE WEALTH OF PRAYER

"Now unto Him that is able to do exceeding abundantly, above all that we can ask or think," what a vision the apostle must have had! How much can a man ask or think? When the deepest convictions of sin are upon him, in his hour of dark despondency, in some perilous pass of life, when fears come upon his soul as on Lake Galilee the storms come, consider how much a man then asks! Or when love swells in his soul, and makes life as full as mountains make the streams in spring, and hope is the sun by day and the moon by night,—in those glorious elate hours when he seems no longer fixed to space and time, but, mounting, as if the body were forgotten by the soul, wings his way through the realm of aspiration and conception, consider how much a man then thinks! The prayers of exiles, of martyrs, of missionaries, of the Waldenses, of the covenanters, of mothers for children gone astray, when with splash of tears, and yearnings that can find no speech, they implore God's mercy upon them,—if some angel, catching them as they were uttered, should drop them down from heaven, what a liturgy would they make!— BEECHER.

THE BELL-ROPE OF HEAVEN

Prayer pulls the rope below and the great bell rings above in the ears of God. Some scarcely stir the bell, for they pray so languidly; others give an occasional pluck at the rope; but he who wins with heaven is the man who grasps the rope boldly, and pulls continuously, with all his might.— SPURGEON.

AN EXAMPLE OF FAITH IN PRAYER

I remember hearing of a boy brought up in an English almshouse. He had never learned to read or write. He only knew the letters of the alphabet. One day a man of God came there, and told the children that if they prayed to God in their trouble, He would send them help. After a time this boy was apprenticed to a farmer. One day he was sent out into the fields to look after some sheep. He was having rather a hard time; so he remembered what the preacher had said, and he thought he would pray to God about it. Some one going by the field heard a voice behind the hedge. They looked to see whose it was, and saw the little fellow on his knees, saying, "A, B, C, D," and so on. The man said, "My boy, what are you doing?" He looked up and said he was praying. "Why, that is not praying; it is only saying the alphabet." He said he did not know just how to pray, but a man once came to the poor-house, who told them that if they called upon God, He would help them. So he thought that if he named over the letters of the alphabet, God would take them and put them together into a prayer, and give him what he wanted. The little fellow was really praying. Sometimes when your child talks, your friends cannot understand what he says, but the mother understands very well. So if our prayer comes right from the heart, God understands our language. —MOODY.

PRAYER OMNIPOTENT

The direct power of prayer is, in a sense, omnipotent. Prayer moves the hand that moves the world. It secures for the believer the resources of divinity. What battles has it not fought! What victories has it not won! What burdens has it not carried! What wounds has it not healed! What griefs has it not assuaged! It is the wealth of poverty, the refuge of affliction; the strength of weakness; the light of darkness. It is the oratory that gives power to the pulpit, it is the hand that strikes down Satan, and breaks the fetters of sin; it turns the scales of fate more than the edge of the sword, the craft of statesmen, or the weight of scepters, it has arrested the wings of time, turned aside the very scythe of death, and discharged heaven's frowning and darkest cloud in a shower of blessings.— GUTHRIE.

A PULPIT PRAYER IN CITY TEMPLE, LONDON

Almighty God, hear the hearts that are full of prayer, that cannot utter their desires on account of the vehemency of their secret emotion. Hear the parent who wonders where the wanderer is, and would offer him a thousand welcomes if he would return. Hear the mother who must live in her sighs, because she dare not put them into speech, so keen and poignant her yearnings after those who are out of the way. Hear Thou the unuttered desires of the penitent; the man who would return if he could find some secret door by which to come stealthily into his Father's dishonored house; find such a way for him Thyself this very day, and make this the birthday of his soul, the genesis of a blessed immortality. Hear us for our loved ones who are sick, Mighty Physician, Tender Nurse, go into all our sick chambers, and by the brightness of Thy presence bring healing to the souls that soon must quit their tenements of clay.

The Lord look upon the old man tottering over his staff, and on the edge of the open grave; the Lord's own fingers touch the cheek of the babe cooing in his cradle. The Lord's eyes be for good upon the bent old woman who has seen the measure of her time and longs for the city of rest. The Lord turn the counsel of every evil man into confusion, and bring him thereby not to ruin; but to contrition! The Lord unsettle the foundation of every iniquitous throne; the Lord baffle the decrees of every wicked empire, and prosper every man who endeavors to do good with simplicity and earnestness!

The Lord hear us in these things! We are always in His arms; may He now draw us more closely to His heart I Amen.—PARKER.

IGNORANT PRAYERS ANSWERED IN LOVE

Look at the case of your own family to-day, and your child shall come and say to you, "Give me your most precious possession." What would be your answer to the little child? Would it be an instant imparting of the gift? Nothing of the kind. Your child shall come to you and say, "Let me go out all to-day, and all to-morrow, and never ask where I am or what I am doing. Now I have asked you, give." What would you say to your seven-year-old little boy who came with that prayer? If ye, then, being children of the night, bewildering shadows, unable to see straight and clear, know how to say "No" under the inspiration of love, how much more may your Father in Heaven say "No" to your poor prayers, your ignorant supplications, your asking for scorpions under the supposition that they are eggs. For the naturalist tells us that the scorpion coils itself up so as to look very much like an egg; hardhearted would be our Father in Heaven, having heard our prayer when we have mistaken a coiled scorpion for an egg, if his answer would be the reply of death.—PARKER.

PREACHING

"The preaching of the cross."—1 Cor. 1:18.

> Would I describe a preacher, each as Paul,
> Were he on earth, would hear, approve and own—
> Paul should himself direct me, I would trace
> His master-strokes, and draw from his design.
> I would express him simple, grave, sincere;
> In doctrine, uncorrupt; in language, plain;
> And plain in manner; decent, solemn, chaste,
> And natural in gesture; much impressed
> Himself, as conscious of his awful charge,
> And anxious mainly that the flock he feeds
> May feel it too. Affectionate in look,'
> And tender in address, as well becomes
> A messenger of grace to guilty men.
> —WILLIAM COWPER.

O! if you could have seen Paul preach, you would not have gone away from the sermon as you do from some of us, with half a conviction that we do not mean what we say. His eyes preached a sermon without his lips, and his lips preached it, not in a cold and frigid manner, but every word fell with an overwhelming power upon the hearts of his hearers. He preached with power, because he was in downright earnest. You had a conviction when you saw him that he was a man who thought he had a work to do, and must do it, and could not contain himself unless he did do it He was the kind of a preacher whom you would expect to see walk down the pulpit stairs, straight into his coffin, and then stand before his God, ready for his last account. Where are the men like that man? I confess I cannot claim that privilege, and I seldom hear a solitary sermon which comes up to the mark in earnest, deep, passionate longing for the souls of men. We have no eyes now like the eyes of the Savior, which could weep over Jerusalem; we have few voices like that earnest, impassioned voice, which seemed perpetually to cry, "O Jerusalem 1 Jerusalem 1 how often would I have gathered thee as a hen gathereth her chickens under her wings, but ye would not." If ministers of the gospel, instead of giving lectures, and devoting a large part of their time to literary and political pursuits, would preach the word of God, and preach it as if they were pleading for their own lives, ah! then, my brethren, we might expect better success.— SPURGEON.

PREACHING THE GOSPEL

I have spoken a great many times in New York city, but I believe that I never preached the gospel here but once. That was twelve or fifteen years ago down at the Tombs. I have spoken a great many times in different parts of the city, but I have never preached the gospel but once. I have tried to arouse Christians up to work. People are in the habit of thinking that anything that is in the way of a religious meeting is the gospel, but they are mistaken. I have had quite a number of letters from Christians complaining because I don't preach the gospel to the people. Now, I believe I was converted years before I knew what the gospel meant. Now the word means "good spell," or in other words "God's spell."

The gospel is good tidings, tidings not of condemnation and sentence, but of pardon and peace. Christ came into the world to bring good news. Did you ever see or hear any one that didn't like to hear good news? The gospel is good tidings of great joy, which shall be to all people, "for unto us is born, in the city of David, a Savior." I don't believe that better news ever fell upon the ears of mortal man, than the news of the gospel. Now any man can preach, but all are not anointed to the preaching of the gospel. Yonder is a man who preaches law, yonder one who preaches philosophy, another science, another ethics, all preachers, but not of the gospel. "The Spirit of the Lord is upon me, because He hath anointed me to preach the gospel to the poor."—MOODY.

THEY MAKE OTHERS FEEL WHO FEEL THEMSELVES

An obscure man rose up to address the French Convention. At close of his oration Mirabeau, the giant genius of the Revolution, turned round to his neighbor, and eagerly asked, "Who is that"? The other, who had been in no way interested by the address, wondered at Mirabeau's curiosity. Whereupon the latter said, "That man will yet ask a great part," and, being asked to explain himself, added, "He speaks as one who believes every word he says." Much of pulpit power under God depends oh that —admits of that explanation, or one allied to it. They make others feel, who feel themselves.—GUTHRIE.

ILLUSTRATIVE PREACHING

Illustrative preaching is intended as well for the unlearned as the learned, for converting the unlettered poor, whose souls are as precious in God's sight as those of philosophers or kings. An humble woman well expressed it, "I like best the likes of scripture." She comprehended best, and was most interested and edified by those passages of the Bible which present abstract truth under concrete forms, and of which we have examples in such expressions of our Lord's as these— "The kingdom of heaven is like unto a grain of mustard seed—unto a treasure—unto a merchant —unto a householder—unto a husbandman—unto a king." A story in a sermon, like a float, keeps it from sinking; like a nail, fastens it in the mind; like the feathers of an arrow makes it strike; and like the barb, makes it stick."—IBID.

LEARNING HOW TO PREACH

If it is your duty, go to preaching the gospel. How shall you learn to preach? Just as the carpenter learns how to be a carpenter. Does he sit down and study books about tools, about hammers and axes? Oh, no! He goes to boring with the bit, and smoothing with the plane, and smiting with the hammer, and striking with the axe; and in this way he gets to be a carpenter. So, the way to learn how to preach the gospel is to preach it.

Yonder is a man who ought to be preaching. He has not been ordained, and he never will be. He could not be, perhaps. It may be he has not brains enough, or time enough, or money enough. But he is ordained of God. Let him preach. Here is another. He may not perhaps be able to round his sentences, or make elegant allusions or fine quotations; and yet he may be able to save a soul from death and hide a multitude of sins. Oh! for five thousand men such as Moody to come out of Chicago, and five thousand George H. Stuarts, to come out from Philadelphia, and five thousand Henry F. Durants to come out from Boston, and preach this glorious gospel, waiting for no other ordination except that which comes from the hand of the Lord Almighty.—TALMAGE.

EXPERIMENTAL PREACHING

There is no such preaching as the experience which a man gives who has just realized the sinfulness of his own soul. I often hear myself outpreached by some new convert who can hardly put words together. Some say experimental preaching is shallow. Shallow! It is as deep as the soul of God.

Young man, when you get a parish don't get discouraged for the first ten years, no matter how poor the work. There is no trade that requires so long an apprenticeship as preaching; and yet there is no trade to which they admit a man so soon, or in which he learns so fast It is easier to study law and become a successful practitioner, it is easier to study medicine and become a successful practitioner, than it is to study the human soul all through,—to know its living forms, and to know the way of talking to it, and coming into sympathy with it

THE APOSTOLIC IDEA OF PREACHING

The apostolic idea of preaching was the secret of the power of the first Christian Church for many hundred years. It is historically true that Christianity did not in its beginning succeed by the force of its doctrines, but by the lives of its disciples. It succeeded first as a light, in accordance with the Master's command. "Let your light so shine before men that they, seeing your good works, may glorify your Father which is in heaven." Make religion attractive by the goodness that men see in you; be so sweet, so sparkling, so buoyant, so cheerful, hopeful, courageous, conscientious and yet not stubborn, so perfectly benevolent and yet not mawkish or sentimental; blossom, ing in everything that is good, a rebuke to everything that is mean or little,—make such men of yourselves that every body who looks upon you may say, "that is a royal good fellow; he has the spirit that I should like to lean upon in time of trouble, or to be a companion with at all times." Build up such a manhood that it shall be winning to men. That is what the early Christians did.

We are to seek to preach, not simply by our own personal experience, but by bringing together one and another m the church, and having the whole life of the church so beautiful in the community that it shall be a constant attraction to win men unceasingly to us and our influence. —BEECHER.

DISHONORING THE BIBLE

It is indeed pitiable, something quite absurdly vain to hear a certain kind of people making out by lame violence, which they mistake for forcible reasoning, that the Bible is an old-world book, a rag out of fashion, not a garment fit for this day's wearing. Some knavish preachers are not ashamed to do this: They have lived on the dear old book, it has kept them and their families in food and lodging these last thirty years, and yet they have nothing good to say about it; they like better the last book which they do not understand, or the last novel which is as hemlock or strychnine to the soul. Thieves they be, knaves with pulpit robes reluctantly thrown over their thievish breasts. Beware of them. They are clever liars, swindlers who look too innocent to be quite guiltless, hirelings who hunger for the pelf. I could respect, in some grim way, the vulgar infidel who blasphemes openly and on purpose, and rejoices in his pitiful bellowing, mistaking the very blatency for courage; but the man in the pulpit who insults the Bible on which he lives, and wriggles out of the profession by which he climbed to the pulpit he dishonors, I charge with worse crimes than those which blackened Barrabus or damned Iscariot.—PARKER.

PRACTICAL PREACHING

A mistake is often made about this matter of practical preaching. If a man denounce the iniquities of his day, he is thought to be a practical preacher. To a certain extent he is entitled to that designation. If I were to denounce theatres (as usually understood), race courses, public houses, gambling houses, I should be thought to be a most practical preacher, and within a given limit,—a very small one, albeit,—I should be preaching practically and usefully. That work needs to be done, must be done. But he, too, is a practical preacher who encourages men to try to be better and do better. He also is a practical preacher who says, "Young man, you failed there, but pluck up your spirits; try again; God bless you; try to do better next time." He also is a practical preacher who recognizes the sufferings of those who come to God's house to hear his word. Sorrow is as great fact as sin. There is not a heart here to-day that has not ached, or that will ache, by-and-by. I take you man for man, pew after pew, and the mourners outnumber those who have had nothing but gladness. The preacher, therefore, is a practical preacher who recognizes that fact, and speaks comfortably, who delivers healing gospels to broken hearts, who deals out bread to the hungry, and who gives the garment of praise for the spirit of heaviness. I often want to hear such a preacher myself; namely, the man who takes the high and bright view of things, who shows me that my pain is for my good, that my loss is the beginning of my riches, that all discipline and chastening, though for the present anything but joyous, will afterward yield me results that will make the soul nobler and tenderer.— PARKER.

PROCRASTINATION

"Seek the Lord while He may be found; call upon Him while He is near."—Isaiah 55:6.

<blockquote>
To-morrow, and to-morrow, and to-morrow,
Creeps in this pretty face from day to day,
To the last syllable of recorded time;
And all our yesterdays have lighted fools
The way to dusty death. Out, out, brief candle!
    —SHAKESPEARE.
</blockquote>

SHAME, PRIDE, OR FEAR

Hungry souls go up and down, to and fro, before Christ's table, when there is bread that will cause that hunger to cease forever, and water that is drawn from the river coming from God's throne; and yet they have gone back, thinking what wife would say, what father would say, what the business partner would say, what gay companions would say. They feel that gnawings of hunger, and, as they look at the spread table, they say, "Oh, how we need this food, but we dare not come and take it." Oh! what is it causes their delay, and keeps them thus back? It is shame, pride, or fear.—BEECHER.

DANGER OF DELAY

Do any of you remember the loss of the vessel called the "Central America?" She was in a bad state, had sprung a leak and was going down, and she therefore hoisted a signal of distress. A ship came close to her, the captain of which asked through the trumpet, "What is the matter?" "We are in bad repair, and are going down: lie by till morning," was the answer. But the captain of the rescue-ship said, "Let me take your passengers on board now." "Lie by till morning," was the answer that came back. Once again the captain cried, "You had better let me take your passengers on board now." "Lie by till morning," sounded through the trumpet About an hour and a half after, the lights were missing, and though no sound was heard, she and all on board had gone down to the fathomless abyss. O unconverted friends, for God's sake do not stay in sin and answer the Spirit's pleadings, "Lie by till morning." To-day, even to-day hear ye toe voice of God.—SPURGEON.

A SAD EXAMPLE OF PROCRASTINATION

A man told me the following story, which I have never forgotten. "When I left home my mother gave me this text: "Seek first the kingdom of God." But I paid no heed to it. I said when I got settled in life, and my ambition to get money was gratified, it would be time enough then to seek the kingdom of God. I went from one village to another and got nothing to do. When Sunday came, I went into a village church, and what was my surprise to hear the minister give out this text, "Seek first the kingdom of God." The text went to toe bottom of my heart I thought that it was only my mother's prayers following me, or that some one must have written to the minister about me. I felt very uncomfortable, and when the meeting was over, I could not get the sermon out of my mind. I went away from that town, and at the end of a week went into another church, and heard the minister give out toe same text, "Seek first the kingdom of God." I felt sure this time it was the prayers of my mother, but I said calmly and deliberately, "No, I must first get wealthy." I went on, and did not go into a church for a few months, but the first place of worship I went into, a third minister preached a sermon from the same text. I tried to drown, to stifle my feelings; tried to get the sermon out of my mind, and resolved that I would keep away from church altogether, and for a few years did keep out of God's house. My mother died, and that text she had given me kept coming up in my mind, and I said I will try to become a Christian. I could not; no sermon ever touches me; "my heart is as hard as a stone."

I heard that story when I was a boy, and after I got to be a man, I went back home, and asked my mother what had become of the man who told it. "Didn't I write to you about him?" she asked. "They have taken him to an insane asylum, and to every one who goes there, he points upward with his finger and says, "Seek first the kingdom of God." There, in the asylum, was that man with his eyes dull with the loss of reason, but the text had sunk into his soul—it had burned down deep.—MOODY.

TEMPORAL VERSUS ETERNAL INTERESTS

As death may happen any day, it is certainly wise to be prepared for it every day. So men make their wills; but, so, alas, they don't mind their souls! This ye should have done, but not have left the other undone. There is no lawyer, but, if you have any property to dispose of, and would not have your death the signal for quarrels and lawsuits and heart burnings, will advise you to make a settlement, nor delay one day to do so. Oh, how much more need to make your peace with God, and prepare your eternal rather than your temporal affairs for death,—to make it all up with Him who is willing to forgive all, and is now tarrying on the road, to give you time to get oil, and go forth with joy to the cry, "Behold the Bridegroom cometh.— GUTHRIE.

PREPARATION FOR A LONG JOURNEY

What if a man going to San Francisco should make preparations for his journey from Brooklyn to Hoboken, and no further. Would you not call him a fool? But here is a man about starting on an everlasting journey, and yet he postpones his preparation until the very last moment of time. The distance from here to the grave is smaller when compared with eternity, than the distance from here to Hoboken is small compared with the thousands of miles between here and San Francisco. Here is a man who thinks only of the three or four yards of human life, and regards not the millions of furlongs stretching out into the infinite.

LOSING THE THRONE

My brother, I am afraid you may lose heaven the way Louis Phillipe lost his empire. The Parisian mob came around the Tuilleries. The national guard stood in defense of the palace, and the commander said to Louis Phillipe, "Shall I fire now? shall I order the troops to fire? With one volley we can clear the place." "No," said Louis Phillipe, "Not yet." A few minutes passed on, and then Louis Phillipe seeing the case was hopeless, said to the general, "Now is the time to fire." "No," said the general, "It is too late now; don't you see the soldiers are exchanging arms with the citizens? It is too late." Down went the throne of Louis Phillipe. Away from the earth went the house of Orleans, and all because the king said, "Not yet, not yet" May God forbid that any of you should adjourn this great subject of religion, and should postpone assailing your spiritual foes until it is too late— too late, you losing a throne in heaven the way that Louis Phillipe lost a throne on earth.—TALMAGE.

PUNISHMENT

"These shall go away into everlasting punishment."—Matthew 25:46.

When, after life is o'er, and we have passed
To our eternal destiny, and fixed for aye
Our dwelling place, in heaven or hell,
If happy we shall be with angel hosts above,
Our joy shall be not all in present peace,
And in the company of souls redeemed;
But in the memory of Christian acts and words
On earth we did and spoke for His name's sake.
But if in hell, We upward lift our hopeless eyes
To plead for those we left behind in sin,
And if, in banishment from God, our course shall end,
Not all our torment shall be in the fiery heat,
Where wailings, gnashing of the teeth and cries
Of pain unceasing shall ascend; but in the recollection
Of our stubborn will which led us to reject the Lord;
To toll the feet of others from the way; to break a mother's heart;
To curse the God who made us, and to crucify
Again the loving Jesus. An awful sentence that—
"Remember thou!" A punishment intense, from which to flee,
Will be impossible.
—CHARLES BENJ. MANLY.

PUNISHMENT PROPORTIONED TO SIN

We sometimes say that punishment should be proportioned to sin. There is a sense in which that is most true and just. It is most true and just with regard to all punishment that comes from the outside. It is a law which must be obeyed by the parent, the magistrate, and every wronged or offended man. But this is by no means the limit of the question. The punishment which a mom inflicts upon himself is infinitely severer than any punishment that can be inflicted upon him. "A wounded spirit who can bear." You remember how you ill-treated that poor child now dead; you saw the anguish of his soul, and he besought you and you would not hear; and now a great distress is come upon you and your bread is very bitter. Who is punishing you? Not the magistrate. Who then? You are punishing yourself. You cannot forgive yourself. The child touches you at every corner, speaks to you in every dream, moans in every cold wind, and lays its thin pale hand upon you in the hours of riot and excitement. You see that ill-used child everywhere; a shadow on the fair horizon; a background to the face of every other child; a ghastly contrast to everything lovely and fair. Time cannot quench the fire. Events cannot throw into dim distance this tragic fact. It surrounds you, mocks you, defies you, and under its pressure you know the meaning of the words, which no mere grammarian can understand, "The wicked shall go away into everlasting punishment."—PARKER.

THE WAGES OF SIN

Did not one who was as near to me almost, as flesh and blood, and who stood high both in church and in business circles, in an evil hour fall into forgeries? When he awoke to the magnitude of the transgression he would take no release, and said, "I have sinned, and I ought to suffer as any other man would suffer who has sinned," he forced a trial upon the court, was sentenced to the penitentiary and went there willingly. He took his place among the prisoners and served there faithfully; but the hand of the Lord was on him, and his child sickened and died, and the government would not remit a day that he might go to the burial of his darling. Months rolled on, and the wife sickened; her very reason languished. That suffering was followed by all-merciful death. Then in this chastening, even the heart of the government relented, and let him go home to the burial of his wife. Since then he has walked a free life, so far as the law is concerned; but he is solitary. He lives as if he were in the center of the great desert of Sahara; for society will not forgive any man who touches its money.—BEECHER.

A WARNING

Some years ago, on a grand jubilee occasion, a distinguished statesman rose up in the presence of assembled thousands, and, in reply to certain calumnious and dishonorable charges raised his hands in the vast assembly, exclaiming, "These hands are clean!" Now, if you or I, or any of our fallen race, did entertain a hope that we could act over this scene before God in judgment, I could comprehend the calm and unimpassioned indifference with which men sit in churches on successive Sabbaths, eye the Cross of Calvary, and listen to the overtures of mercy. Are these matters with which you have nothing to do? If, indeed, you have no sins to answer for; if before this world's great assize, you are prepared not only to plead, but to prove your innocence; if conscience accuses you in nothing and excuses you in everything, then sleep on, in God's name, sleep on, and take your rest. But when the heavens over men are clothed in thunders, and hell yawns beneath their feet, and both God's law and their own conscience condemn them, such indifference is madness I Beware! Play with no fire; least of all, with fire unquenchable. Play with no edged sword; least of all, with that which justice sheathed in a Savior's bosom. Delay by the mouth of no pit; least of all, on the brink of a bottomless one, the smoke of whose torment goeth up forever and ever.—GUTHRIE.

"SOWING THE TARES"

I was at the Paris exhibition in 1867, and I noticed there a little oil painting, only about a foot square, and the face was the most hideous I have ever seen. On the paper attached to the painting were the words, "Sowing the Tares," and the face looked more like a demon's than a man's. As he sowed these tares, up came serpents and reptiles, and they were crawling up on his body, and all around were wolves and other wild animals prowling in them. I have seen that picture many times since. Ah, the reaper is coming. If you sow to the flesh, you must reap the flesh.— MOODY.

"LIKE THE CHAFF"

The ungodly "are like the chaff which the wind driveth away." Where—where—where? Where are they driven? The man is in health, the sun shines, the sky is calm, the world is still about him. Suddenly there is seen a little cloud the size of a man's hand. A little signal overtakes him. The hurricane begins to rise, but first it is only a faint breath. The wicked man feels the cold air blowing on him, but he screens it with the physician, and he thinks that surely he shall live. The storm is on. God hath decreed it, and man cannot stay it. The breath becomes a wind, the wind a storm, the storm a howling hurricane. His soul is swept away. To go to Heaven on angels wings is a glorious thing; but to be swept out of this world with the wicked is an awful thing—to be carried, not on wings of cherubs, but on the eagle wings of the wind; to be borne, not by yon songsters up to their feathered seats, but to be carried away in the midst of a howling tempest by grim fiends.—SPURGEON.

GOOD ADVICE

In order to hold yourselves masters of your appetites, begin early. It is no use for a man forty-five years of age beginning to say he is going to turn over a new leaf; the leaves won't be turned then. I think, perhaps, I may be speaking discouragingly to some man who is making at that time of life a resolution to do better. Well, to resolution, to perseverance, to devout energy, it is possible, but it is not easy. Young man, lay down your cigar; it will do you no good. Throw away your pipe; it does not make you manly; it only makes you a nuisance to other and better people; and don't touch strong drink of any kind whatever. This is the testimony that I have to bear: that he who gives way to these things in his youth is committing suicide by inches. He is taking away his will-power, he is dulling his finest sensibilities. It does not tell upon him all at once; he may live to be an old man and say: "It is a very slow poison." What he might have been he never thinks of; he only sees what he is, a tough, much-enduring man; whereas, he might have been a very prince, and king, and guide, and friend among the highest classes of the land. Let me ask you to attend to the discipline of saying "No." I love to see the practice of manly sports of the right kind: running, leaping, swimming, and divers gymnastic exercises. I rejoice exceedingly in all these athletic pastimes, and in all these disciplinary sports and enjoyments. They have a great purpose to serve, but there is still a higher discipline—a discipline of the soul; a discipline which enables one to look at a bodily advantage and say: "I will not touch it;" the discipline which enables a man to receive an invitation, on gilt-edged paper and scented, to spend an evening with sinners in their gluttony and their wine bibbing, and that enables him to put it into the fire.—PABKER.

RESURRECTION

"The hour is coming in which all that are in the graves shall hear His voice, and shall come forth."—John 5:28, 29.

> The seed, the insentient seed,
> Buried beneath the earth,
> Starts from its dusty bed,
> Responsive to the breath of spring,
> And covers mead and mountain,
> Fields and forests, with its life.
> Myriads of creatures, too, that lay
> As dead as dust on every inch of ground,
> Touched by the vernal ray,
> Spring from their little graves, and sport
> On beauteous wings in fields of sunny air.
> Shall this be so? shall plants and worms
> Come forth to life again? And, oh, shall man
> Descend into the grave to rise no more?
> Shall he, the master of this world,
> Image and offspring of the fontal life,
> "Through endless ages sleep in dust?
>   -THOMAS.

DEATH A SLEEP, RESURRECTION A WAKING

On a summer's day, the gentle western wind brings in all the sweets of the field and garden; and the child, overtasked by joy, comes back weary, and climbs for sport into the mother's lap; and before he can sport, he feels the balm of rest stealing over him, and lays his curly head back upon her arm;

and look! he goes to sleep; hush! he has gone to sleep; and all the children stand smiling. How beautiful it is to see a child drop asleep upon its mother's arm! And it is said of one, "He fell asleep in Jesus." Is there anything so high, so noble, so divine, as the way in which the New Testament speaks of dying? How near death is, and how beautiful!

If you have lost your companions, children, friends, you have not lost them. They followed the Pilot They went through airy channels, unknown and unsearchable, and they are with the Lord; and you are going to be with Him too. I die to go, not to Jerusalem, but to the New Jerusalem. I die, not to wait in the rock-ribbed sepulchre, which shall hold me sure; I die, that when this body is dropped I shall have a place, in the inward fullness of my spiritual power, with the Lord. "Because He lives, I shall live again, also."—BEECHER.

THE MASTER OF THE GRAVE

Christ is the Master of the grave. Just outside of the gate of the city of Nain, Death and Christ measured lances; and when the young man rose, Death dropped. Now we are sure of our resurrection. Oh, what a scene it was when that young man came back! The mother never expected to hear him speak again. She never thought that he would kiss her again. How the tears started, and how her heart throbbed as she said, "Oh, my son, my son, my son!" And that scene is going to be repeated. It is going to be repeated ten thousand times. These broken family circles have got to come together. These extinguished household lights have got to be rekindled. There will be a stir in the family lot in the cemetery, and there will be a rush into life at the command, "Young man, I say unto thee, arise!" As the child shakes off the dust of the tomb, and comes forth fresh and fair, and beautiful, and you throw your arms around it and press it to your heart, angel to angel will repeat the story of the resurrection at Nain, "He delivered him to his mother."

O ye troubled souls! O ye who have lived to see every prospect blasted, peeled, scattered, consumed! wait a little. The seed-time of tears will become the wheat harvest. In a clime cut of no wintry blast, under a sky palled by no hurtling tempest, and amidst redeemed ones that weep not, that part not, that die not, friend will come to friend, and kindred will join kindred, and the long procession that marches the avenues of gold will lift up their palms as again and again it is announced that the same one who came to the relief of the stricken widow of Nain, to the relief of the weeping sisters of Bethany, has come to the relief of many a maternal heart, and repeated the wonders of resurrection. —TALMAGE.

A JOYFUL DOCTRINE

The doctrine of the resurrection is full of joy to the bereaved. It clothes the grave with flowers and wreathes the tomb with unfading laurel. The sepulchre shines with a light brighter than the sun, and death grows fair, as we say, in full assurance of faith. "I know my brother shall arise again." Bent from the ignoble shell, the pearl is gone to deck the crown of the "Prince of Peace." Buried beneath the sod, the seed is preparing to bloom in the King's garden.—SPURGEON.

A WRONG VIEW OF DEATH

We ought not to look upon death as we do. Bishop Heber has written of a dead friend!

> "Thou art gone to the grave, but we will not deplore thee,
> Though sorrow and darkness encompass the tomb;
> Thy Savior has passed through its portals before thee,
> And the lamp of His love is thy guide through the gloom."

The roll is being called, and one after another is being summoned away, but if their names are there, if we know that they are saved, how sweet it is, after they have left us, to think that we shall meet them by and by; that we shall see them in the mom when the night has worn away.

During the late war a young man lay on a cot, and they heard him say, "Here, here!" and some one went to his cot and wanted to know what he wanted, and he said, "Hark! hush! don't you hear them?" "Hear who?" was asked, "They are calling the roll of heaven," he said, and pretty soon he answered, "Here!" and he was gone. If our names are in the Book of Life, by and by at the trumpet call of the resurrection morning, when the name is called, we can say with Samuel, "Here, Lord Jesus," and fly away to meet Him.—MOODY.

A MATCHLESS CHANGE

Who saw the rolling waves stand up a rocky wall; who saw the water of Cana flow out rich purple wine; who saw Lazarus's festering corpse, with health glowing on its cheek, and its arms enfolding sisters ready to faint with joy, saw nothing to match the change the grave shall work on these mouldering bones. Sown in corruption, they shall rise in incorruption, mortal putting on immortality. How beautiful they shall be! Never more shall hoary time write age on a wrinkled brow. The whole terrible troupe of diseases cast with sin into hell, the saints shall possess unfading beauty, and enjoy a perpetual youth; a pure soul shall be mated with a worthy partner in a perfect body, and an angel form shall lodge an angel mind.—GUTHRIE.

REST

"There remaineth therefore a rest to the people of God."—Heh. 4:9.

We are but children crying here upon a mother's breast,
For life and peace and blessedness, and for eternal rest!
Bless God I hear a still small voice, above life's clamorous din,
Saying, "Faint not, O weary one, thou yet mayst enter in;
That city is prepared for those who well do win the fight,
Who tread the wine-press till its blood hath washed their garments white;
Within it is no darkness, nor any baleful flower
Shall there oppress thy weeping eyes with stupifying power.
It lieth calm within the light of God's peace-giving breast,
Its walls are called Salvation, the city's name is Rest."
—ANON.

DESIRE FOR REST

What has been, and is now, one of the strongest feelings in the human heart? Is it not to find some better place, some lovlier spot, than we have now? It is for this that men are seeking everywhere; and yet, they can have it, if they will; but instead of looking down, they must look up to find it. As men grow in knowledge, they vie with each other more and more in making their homes attractive, but the brightest home on earth is but an empty barn, compared with the mansions that are in the skies.

What is it that we look for at the decline and close of life? Is it not some sheltered place, some quiet spot, where, if we cannot have constant rest, we may at least have a foretaste of what perfect rest is to be. What was it that led Columbus, not knowing what would be his fate, across the unsailed western seas, if it was not the hope of finding a better country? This it was that sustained the hearts of the Pilgrim Fathers, driven from their native land by persecution, as they faced a rock-bound, savage coast, with an unexplored territory beyond. They were cheered and upheld by the hope of reaching a free and fruitful country, where they could be at rest and worship God in peace. Somewhat similar is the Christian's hope of heaven. —MOODY.

THE CHRISTIAN'S LIFE NOT ONE OF REST

The life of a Christian is not one of rest. He who is converted, believes, and is thereby savingly united to Christ, has, to use the words of Nehemiah, "a great work to do." He enters on a harder task than Gideon's. His enemies, paralyzed with terror, flying like a flock of sheep that barking dogs pursue, fell without an attempt at resistance. Not so does Satan yield. He makes desperate efforts to rally his scattered forces, and recover the ground he has lost. By no means easily expelled, he lurks in our habits and hides in the recesses of our hearts. Now a cunning serpent, and now a roaring lion; at one time with devilish craft he proposes terms of peace, and at another, seeking not to deceive, but to cast us into despair, he comes forth, boastful as Goliath, to defy the armies of the living God. And even when he flies, as the apostle assures us he will do if we resist him, he flies like the ancient Parthians—fighting all the while, and with the fiery darts he shoots, putting the believer's peace in jeopardy, and making his armor ring.

To conquer sin is work unceasing, and not at all easy. I know a weed which, more than any other which infests the ground, gardeners and husbandmen find it hard to exterminate. Shooting its long, knotted fibres under the surface, spreading in all soils, whether rich or poor, with unexampled rapidity, it survives being crushed beneath the heel, or cut into morsels with the spade; and, tenacious of life, springs again, if the smallest portion of its root is left in the ground. Such is sin! With an enemy like this can we have any cessation from work?—GUTHRIE.

DANGER OF RESTFUL EASE

Dangers are in very many cases blessings in disguise, They prevent us from drowsiness in spiritual matters. You never read that Christian went to sleep when lions were in the way; he never slept when he was going through the river Death, or when he was in Giant Despair's castle, or when he was fighting with Apollyon. Poor creature! he almost wished he could sleep then.

But when he had got half way up the Hill Difficulty, and came to a pretty little arbor, in he went, and sat down, and began to read his roll. O, how he rested himself! How he unstrapped his sandals and rubbed his weary feet! Very soon his mouth was open, his arms hung down, and he was fast asleep. Again, the enchanted ground was a very easy, smooth place, and liable to send the pilgrim to sleep. You remember Bunyan's descriptions of some of the arbors. "Then they came to an arbor, warm, and promising much refreshing to the weary pilgrims; for it was finely wrought above head, beautified with greens and furnished with benches and settees. It had also in it a soft couch, where the weary might lean."

Oh, depend upon it, it is in easy places that men shut their eyes, and wander into the dreamy land of forgetfulness. Take care, thou who art full of gladness. There is no season in which we are so likely to fall asleep as that of high enjoyment. The disciples went to sleep after they had seen Christ transfigured on the mountain top. Rest not, O Christian, while souls are being lost, while men are being damned, while hell is being peopled, while Christ is being dishonored, while the devil is grinning at thy sleepy face; while demons are dancing round thy slumbering carcass, and telling it in hell that a Christian is asleep!— SPURGEON.

IDLENESS NOT REST

Idleness is not rest. Idleness is not happiness. Rest is. The poor man with industry is happier than the rich man in indolence. Labor makes the one more manly, while riches unmans the other. The slave is often happier than the master, who is nearer undone by license than his vassal by toil. Luxurious couches, plushy carpets from Oriental looms, pillows of eider-down, carriages contrived with cushions and springs to make motion imperceptible,—is the indolent master of these as happy as the slave who wove the carpet, the Indian who hunted the northern flock, or the servant who drives the pampered steeds? Let those who envy the gay revels of city idlers, and pine for their masquerades, their routs, and their operas, experience for a week the lassitude of their society, the unarousable torpor of their life when not under a fiery stimulus, their desperate ennui and restless somnolency, and they would gladly flee from their haunts as from a land of cursed enchantment. —BEECHER.

REWARD

"Be thou faithful unto death, and I will give thee a crown of life."—Rev. 2:10.

"The season will come and is coming,
When the Christian shall lay down the cross,
And receive the reward from his glorified Lord,
    Feel joy without measure.
    Exchange gain for pleasure,
Obtain gain for loss."
        —CHAS. BENJ. MANLY,

REWARD FOR UNAPPRECIATED LABOR

Cheer up men and women of unappreciated services. You will get your reward, if not here, hereafter. When Charles Wesley comes up to judgment, and the thousands of souls which were wafted into glory through his songs shall be enumerated, he will take his throne. When John Wesley will come up to judgment his name will be mentioned in connection with the salvation of millions of souls brought to God through the Methodism which he founded, and he will take his throne. But between the two thrones of John Wesley and Charles Wesley, there will be a throne higher than either, on which shall sit Susannah Wesley, who with maternal consecration in Epworth Rectory, started those two souls on their mission of sermon and song through all following ages. Oh, what a day that will be for many who rocked Christian cradles with weary feet, who patched worn-out garments and darned socks, and with a small income made the children comfortable for the winter. What a day that will be for those to whom the world gave the cold shoulder, and called them nobodies, and begrudged them the least recognition, and who, weary and worn, and sick, fainted by the brook Besor. Oh, that will be a mighty day when the Son of David shall distribute among them the garlands the crowns, the scepters, the chariots, the thrones. And then it shall be found out that all who on earth served God in inconspicuous spheres received just as much reward as those who filled the earth with uproar of achievement. Then they shall understand the height, the depth, the length, the breadth, the pillared and domed significance of that verse: "As his part is that goeth down to the battle, so shall his part be that tarrieth by the stuff."—TALMAGE.

THE LIGHT WILL SOON BREAK

Last night I saw a faint yellow light struggling with feeble timidity against some angry clouds; they gathered against the light as if determined to shut it out; and the pale moon seemed too languid for resistance, but the breeze came to help her; the thickening clouds were broken, and the moon seemed to take heart; brighter and brighter were her mild beams, until at last she stood up in the southern sky, the clouds all gone, like an angel watching from afar the flowers which the sun had just forsaken. So shall it be with our cloudy life, if we be God's children, the clouds are not permanent They are but elevated shadows. The true light will pierce them, melt them, scatter them, and we shall stand out distinct as stars, lighter than ever cloud ascended, renewed in lustre by the infinite glory of God.—PARKER.

THE CHRISTIAN'S REWARD

Am I poor? He cannot be poor to whom God's angels come every day and every night Have I no riches here? I have all that every man owns on this earth, and all that God owns besides. I am an heir of God. I am joint heir with Jesus Christ.

You say, "That is a hifalutin notion." It is not. I am myself a witness, and I testify that this is so. I do own the beauty and the glory of this world because 1 am a child of God, and as such, I am the heir of my Father. There is not a bird that flies that is not mine. There is not an insect that lives and enjoys its brief space of life that is not mine. There is not a mountain-top that is not mine. There is nothing that glows in the seasons that is not mine. The very drapery of the heavens is mine. He is yours whom you love, and he cannot keep himself. And this is our re-ward.—BEECHER. '

THE BRIGHTEST HONORS OF HEAVEN

Others may have filled the world with the breath of their name; he has helped to fill Heaven; others may have won an earthly renown; but he who, a Christian himself, has sought to make others Christians—who, reaching the rock himself, draws another, a perishing child, friend, brother, neighbor, up—plucked from the flood himself, pulls another out—who has leaped into the depths that he might rise with a pearl, and set it lustrous in Jesus' crown— he is the man who shall wear Heaven's brightest honors, and to whom, before all else, the Lord will say: "Well done, good and faithful servant, enter thou into the joy of thy Lord."—GUTHRIE.

REWARD OF GOODNESS SOMETIMES IMMEDIATE

Occasionally a benevolent action wrought in faith brings with it an instantaneous recompense in kind; therein Providence is seen as smiling upon the deed. The late John Andrew Jones, a poor Baptist minister, whilst walking in Cheapside, was appealed to for help by some one he knew. He had but a shilling in the world, and poised it in his mind to give or not to give? The greater distress of his acquaintance prevailed, and he gave his all, walking away with the sweet remembrance of the promise: "He that hath pity upon the poor, lendeth unto the Lord, and that which he hath given will He pay him again." He had not gone a hundred yards further before he met a gentleman who said: "Ah, Mr. Jones, I am indeed glad to see you. I have had this sovereign in my waistcoat pocket for a week past for some poor minister, and you may as well have it." Mr. Jones was wont to add, when telling the story: "If I had not stopped to give relief, I should have missed the gentleman and the sovereign too."—SPURGEON.

HEAVEN A PLACE OF REWARD

Heaven is the place of victory and triumph. This is the battle-field; there is the triumphal procession. This is the land of the sword and the spear; that is the land of the wreath and the crown. Oh, what a thrill of joy will shoot through the hearts of all the blessed when their conquests will be made complete in Heaven; when death itself, the last of foes, shall be slain, and Satan dragged as captive at the chariot wheels-of Christ.—MOODY.

RICHES

"How hardly shall they that have riches enter into the kingdom of God."—Luke 18:24.

Gold and silver like the snow
    Quickly pass away;
Like the curtained clouds of summer,
    Enduring not a day;
Like the early dew of morning,
    Drunken by the sun;
Or the maddened hill-side torrent,
    Whose course is quickly run.
But the grace of Christ, our Savior,
    Bringeth riches more
Than the tongue of man can utter,
    And of wealth a store
Like the river, failing never
    Flowing evermore.
        —CHAS. BENJ. MANLY.

ADVERSITY A BLESSING SOMETIMES

I don't believe we would have had such a blessing in New York during these meetings, if it had not been for these hard times. When men get their millions, and hoard them up, I think it is the very best thing that can happen to them to have the Lord come and take their riches away. If a man lends his money to the Lord, in maintaining good works, he will never lose it. People say that such a man died worth so many millions. It doesn't make any difference how much a man accumulates, he can't die worth anything, for he leaves it here. He is not worth a penny, if he has not laid it up in heaven, where thieves do not break through and steal.—MOODY.

DANGER OF RICHES

The danger and deceitful influence of riches, their tendency to turn our thoughts away from another world, and drown such concern for the soul as providences or preachers may have awakened, in the cup of pleasure, is awfully expressed in the saying of the Lord, "It is easier for a camel to go through the eye of a needle, than for a rich man to enter into the kingdom of God." Dr. Johnson put the point well when, on Garrick showing him his beautiful mansion and grounds. The great man and moralist laid his hand gently on the player's shoulder, and said, "Ah, David, David, these are the things which make a death-bed terrible!"—GUTHRIE.

"A POOR RICH MAN."

A man may have every comfort and luxury here, and yet come to a wretched future. It is no sin to be rich. It is a sin not to be rich, if we can be honestly. I wish I had five hundred thousand dollars—I suppose I might as well make it a million—I see so much suffering and trial every day, that I say again and again, I wish I had the money to relieve it. But alas for the man who has nothing but money I Dives' house had a front door and a back door, and they both opened into eternity. Sixty seconds after Dives was gone, of what use were his horses? he could not ride them; of what use his rich viands? he could not open his clenched teeth to eat them; of what use his fine linen shirts! he could not wear them. The poorest man who stood along the road watching the funeral procession of Dives owned more of this world than the dead gormandizer. The future of the other world was all the darker because of the brightness of this. Who of you will take Dives' fine home, and costly plate, and dazzling equipage, and kennel of blooded dogs, if his eternity must b6 thrown in with it?

The Indian who for a string of beads sells as much territory as will make a State, is wise compared with a man who for the trinkets of earth barters heaven.—TALMAGE.

SHAM GENEROSITY

Oftentimes you will find men who have been penurious all their lives, and who have amassed a fortune, attempting to buy respect in their old age.

Sometimes they do it by making their will, and letting it be known what they are going to do. That is an exquisite piece of trickery. Where a man wants to keep his money, and also wants to have the credit of giving it away, he holds on to it, and lets it be known that he is going to give $250,000 for benevolent purposes,—$10,000 here, and $20,000 there, $50,000 somewhere else, and so on. There are many men that are going to be very generous when they die. Dead men are always generous. They keep their money while they live, and only give it away when they no longer own it. When men are surrounded by all that earth can give them,—by position, by circumstance, by plenary physical blessings,—how, after all, do they long for more! How pitious it is to see them!—BEECHER.

AVOID ANXIETY FOR RICHES

Do not be over-anxious about riches. Get as much of true wisdom and goodness as you can; but be satisfied with a very moderate portion of this world's good. Riches may prove a curse as well as a blessing.

I was walking through an orchard looking about me, when I saw a low tree laden more heavily with fruit than the rest. On a nearer examination, it appeared that the tree had been dragged to the very earth, and broken by the weight of its treasures. "Oh," said I, gazing on the tree, "here lies one who has been ruined by his riches."

In another part of my walk, I came up with a shepherd who was lamenting the loss of a sheep that lay mangled and dead at his feet. On inquiring about the matter, he told me that a strange dog had attacked the flock, that the rest of the sheep had got away through a hole in the hedge, but that the ram now dead had more wool on his back than the rest, and the thorns of the hedge held him fast till the dog had worried him. "Here is another," said I, "ruined by his riches."

At the close of my ramble, I met a man hobbling along on two wooden legs, leaning on two crutches. "Tell me," said I, "my poor fellow, how you came to lose your legs." "Why, sir," said he, "in my younger days, I was a soldier. With a few comrades, I attacked a party of the enemy, and overcame them, and we began to overload ourselves with spoil. I burdened myself with as much as I could carry. We were pursued. My companions escaped, but I was overtaken and so cruelly wounded, that I only saved my life afterwards by losing my legs. It was a bad affair, sir, but it is too late to repent of it now." "Ah, friend," thought I, "like the fruit tree and the mangled sheep, you may date your downfall to your possessions. It was your riches that ruined you."—SPURGEON.

SABBATH

"Remember the Sabbath day to keep it holy."—Ex. 20:8.

> Now let ns repose from our care and our sorrow,
> Let all that is anxious and sad pass away;
> The rough cares of life lay aside till to-morrow,
> And let us be tranquil and happy to-day.
> —JAMES EDMESTON.

THE LORD'S DAY IN PARIS

Let my readers fancy that as they pass on their way to the house of God, they see almost all the shops in their native town or village standing open, with men and women buying and selling, and they have an idea of the desecration of the Lord's day in Paris. Th6 tide and toil of business does not cease in very many cases till night brings rest to its weary slaves. On returning from evening service, I have seen them still behind the counter, chained to the oar; and, in not a few instances playing cards when business was slack in the shop. A visit to Paris would convince the working classes that those are their worst friends who attempt to divest the first day of the week of that holiness which, as all experience proves, affords the only security for rest and repose to the sons of toil.— GUTHRIE.

THE MEANNESS OF THE SABBATH BREAKERS

How unutterly mean is the behavior of the Sabbath breaker. It is as though a man had a large estate, and he said to his employees: "Now, I will give you to-day for yourselves—you need not toil a particle;" and then, at the close of day, the employer should find out that they had been stealing out of the corn-crib, not content with the rest he had given them. Just so those do who, when God tells them to rest, and gives them an opportunity to rest, employ the hours for their own enjoyment, neglecting, or entirely overlooking the fact that God all the time on the Sabbath day is just as busy for them as He is on any other day. Their corn is growing just as rapidly on Sabbath as 'on Monday, Tuesday, Wednesday, Thursday, Friday or Saturday. Their bonds and mortgages are bringing just as much interest. Although God has given them a day of rest, He has not taken His hand from their worldly interests.—TALMAGE.

HILLS OF LIGHT AND JOY

Through the week we go down into the valleys of care and shadow. Our Sabbaths should be hills of light and joy in God's presence; and, as time rolls by, we shall go on from mountain top to mountain top, till at last we catch the glory of the gate, and enter in, to go no more out forever.

ADDRESSED TO THE CHURCH AT A WEDNESDAY NIGHT LECTURE

Let us interrupt the flow of the week, and rear up another Sabbath in the middle of it. And, as those who swim mighty streams do stop, panting, to rest upon some midway rock ere they plunge again into the tide, so let us rest here, lifted up above the tumult of earthly care, and gain strength, before we go down into the dark ford, for the farther shore—the Sabbath.—BEECHER.

SABBATH VIEWS OF HEAVEN

When a gentleman was inspecting a house in Newcastle, with a view to buying it as a residence, the landlord took him to the upper window, expatiated on the extensive prospect, and added, "You can see Durham Cathedral from this window on a Sunday." "Why on Sunday above any other day?" inquired our friend, with some degree of surprise. The reply was conclusive enough. "Because on that day there is no smoke from those tall chimneys." Blessed is the Sabbath to us when the earth-smoke of care and turmoil no longer beclouds our view; then can our souls full often behold the goodly land, and the city of the New Jerusalem.—SPURGEON.

SELF-DENIAL

"Whosoever will come after me, let him deny himself and take up his cross and follow Me."—Mark 8:34.

> Would'st thou inherit life with Christ on high?
> Then count the cost and know
> That here on earth below '
> Thou needs must suffer with thy Lord, and die.
> We reach that gain, to which all else is loss,
> But through the cross!
> —SIMON DACH.

RELIGION REQUIRES SELF-DENIAL

Religion, in one sense, is a life of self-denial, just as husbandry, in one sense is a life of death. You go and bury a seed and that is husbandry; but you bury one, that you may reap a hundred fold. Self-denial does not belong to religion as characteristic of it; it belongs to human life. The lower nature must always be denied when you are trying to reach a higher sphere. It is no more necessary to be self-denying to be a Christian, than it is to be an artist, or to be an honest man, or to be a man at all, in distinction from a brute. Of all joyful, smiling, ever-laughing experiences, there are none like those which spring from true religion.—BEECHER.

OUR EXAMPLE OF SELF-DENIAL

Alexander, when his army grew sluggish because laden with the spoils of their enemies, to free them from this incumbrance, commanded all his own baggage to be set on fire, that when they saw the king himself devote his rich treasures to the flames they might not murmur if their mite and pittance were consumed also. So, if Christ had taught us contempt of the world, and had not given us an instance of it in His own person, His doctrine had been less powerful and effective. But what an example we now find in Him, since he had not where to lay His head in life, nor a rag to cover Him in death, nor anything but a borrowed grave in burial. What manner of persons ought we all to be in unselfishness when we have such a Lord! He hath not said to us in matters of self-denial, "Take up thy cross and go," but "Come, take up thy cross and follow Me." Well may the soldiers endure hardness when the King himself roughs it among us, and suffers more than the meanest private in our ranks.—SPURGEON.

SELF-DENYING LIVES

How grand it is, amid the selfishness of the world, to find such generous deeds! The Moravian missionaries were told that they could not enter the lazarettos where the lepers were dying unless they stayed there. "Then," they said, "We will go and stay there." They went in to nurse the sick and perished. Yon have read the life of pure-hearted Elizabeth Fry, toiling among the degraded. But the full biographies of the world's martyrs will never be written. The firemen in our cities who have rescued people from blazing buildings; the sailors who have helped the passengers off the wreck, themselves perishing; the nurses who have waited upon the sick in yellow fever and cholera hospitals, and sunk down to death from exhaustion; the Christian men who, on the battlefield, have administered to the fallen amid rattling canister and bursting shell; the Christian women who have gone down through haunts of shame on errands of mercy, defended by no human arm, but looked after by that God who, with his lightnings, would have struck to hell any who dared to do them harm! —TALMAGE.

Selfishness is sin. Self-indulgence is criminal. A soul filled with self has no room for God; and like the inn of Bethlehem, given to lodge meaner guests, a heart full of pride has no chamber, within which Christ may be born. "in us the hope of glory." How rare a virtue is self-sacrifice! What can be more sad than to see the value a woman sets on trinkets, the pride with which she shows and wears her jewels, while Jesus has no preciousness in her eyes? What fools people are! They set more value on some glittering bits of glass or stone than oh a crown of glory!—they care more in this dying body for the perishable casket than for the immortal jewel which it holds. —GUTHRIE.

SIN

"To him that knoweth to do good, and doeth it not, to him it is sin."—James 4:17.

Sin is the living worm, the lasting fire;
Hell soon would lose its heat, could sin expire.
—JOHN BUNYAN.

LITTLE SINS

It is high time to get out of your sins. You say, "I have committed no great transgressions." But are you not aware that your life has been sinful? The snow comes down on the Alps flake by flake, and it is so light that you may hold it on the tip of your finger without feeling any weight; but the flakes gather; they compact, until some day a traveler's foot starts the slide, and it goes down in an avalanche, crushing to death the villagers. So the sins of your youth, and the sins of your manhood, and the sins of your womanhood may have seemed only slight inaccuracies, or trifling divergences from the right—so slight that they are hardly worth mentioning, but they have been piling up and piling up, packing together and packing together, until they make a mountain of sin, and one more step of your foot in the wrong direction may slide down upon you an avalanche of ruin and condemnation.—TALMAGE.

SIN IS CRUEL

Sin is not only strong to seduce, but heartless to sustain its victims. It will exhaust your means, teach you to despise the God of your fathers, and then when the inevitable disaster of wickedness begins to overwhelm you, it will abandon whom it has debauched. When at length, death gnaws at your bones, and knocks at your heart, when staggering and worn out, your courage wasted, your hope gone, your purity, and long, long ago your peace— will he who first enticed your steps serve your extremity with one office of kindness? Will he stay your head, cheer your dying agony with one word of hope, or light the way for your coward steps to the grave, or weep when you are gone, or send one pitiful scrap to your desolate family? What reveler wears crape for a dead drunkard? What gang of gamblers ever intermitted a game for the death of a companion? What harlot weeps for a harlot? What debauchee mourns for a debauchee? They would carouse at your funeral, and gamble at your funeral. If one flush more of pleasure were to be had by it, they would drink shame and ridicule to your memory out of your own skull, and roar in bacchanal revelry over your damnation! Oh! the cruel heartlessness of sin!—BEECHER.

THE POWER OF A SINGLE SIN

There was but one crack in the lantern, and the wind has found it out and blown out the candle. How great a mischief one unguarded point of character may cause us. One spark blew up the magazine, and shook the whole country for miles around. One leak sank the vessel and drowned all on board. One wound may kill the body; one sin destroy the soul.—SPURGEON.

SINS ACCUMULATE

Sins seldom come alone; where there is room for one devil, seven other spirits more wicked than himself will find a lodging. We may say of sins as Longfellow says of birds of prey, in his Song of Hiawatha.—.

> "Never stoops the soaring vulture
> On his quarry in the desert,
> On the sick or wounded bison,
> But another vulture watching,
> . From his high aerial look-out
> Sees the downward plunge and follows,
> And a third pursues the second,
> Coming from the invisible ether,
> First a speck, and then a vulture,
> Till the air is dark with pinions."
> —IBID.

SALVATION FROM SIN.

As certain as we are lost in sin, so certain can Christ gave us from our sins. He will save us if we will let Him. A story is told of Rowland Hill, the great preacher. Lady Ann Erskine was passing by in her carriage, and she asked her coachman who that was that was drawing such a large assembly. He replied that it was Rowland Hill. "I have heard a good deal about him," she said, "drive up near the crowd." Mr. Hill soon saw her, and saw that she belonged to the aristocracy. He stopped all at once in the middle of his discourse and said, "My friends, I have something for sale." This astonished his hearers. "Yes, I have, something for sale; it is the soul of Lady Ann Erskine. Is there any one here who will bid for her soul? Ah, do I hear a bid? Who bids? Satan bids. Satan, what will you give for her soul? "I will give riches, honor, and pleasure." But stop; do I hear another bid? Yes, Jesus Christ bids. Jesus, what will you give for her soul? "I will give eternal life." Lady Ann Erskine, you have heard the two bids, which will you take?" And Lady Ann fell on her knees, and cried out, "I will have Jesus." So may it be with you.—MOODY.

A DISEASE OF THE HEART

Like snow drift when it has leveled the church-yard mounds, and glistening in the winter sun, lies so pure and fair and beautiful above the dead, who fester and rot below, a very plausible profession, wearing the semblance of innocence, may conceal from human eyes the foulest heart-corruption. The grass grows green upon a mountain that holds a volcano in its bowels. Behind the rosy cheek, and soft lustrous eye of beauty, how often does there lurk a deadly disease, the deadliest of all! Even so sin has its seat within. It is a disease of the heart, and the worst of all heart complaints.

The most advanced saint is not altogether free from the bondage of sin. Sin is the greatest folly, and the sinner the greatest fool in the world. Think of a man purchasing momentary pleasure at the cost of endless pain. Think of a dying man living as if he were never to die. Think of a man risking eternity on the uncertain chance of surviving another year.—GUTHRIE.

THE EFFECTS OF SIN

Have you ever watched the deteriorating effects of sin even upon the personal appearance? Take a youth of extreme beauty, and let him, little by little, be led into wicked practices; in proportion as he is so led, will the register of his descent be written upon his face, and upon his whole attitude and manners. Quite unperceptibly, I admit, but with awful exactness and depth. The eyes, once so clear and steady in look, will be marked by suspicion, uncertainty, or timidity of movement; their glances will not be like sun rays darting through thick foliage, but rather like a dark lantern turned on skillfully to see what is happening here and there, but throwing no light on the man who holds it. And strange lines will be woven around the mouth; and the lips, so well cut, so guileless and generous, will be tortured into ugliness and sensual enlargement; and the voice, once so sweet, so ringing, the very music of a character unstained and fearless, will contract some mocking tones, and give itself up to a rude laughter, partly deceitful and partly defiant. All this will not happen in one day. Herein is the subtlety of evil. If you do not see the youth for years you may be shocked when you miss the fine simplicity and noble bearing which you associated with the name. It is the spot of leprosy on a "forehead once so open and unwrinkled, and it will grow and spread and deepen until there will be no place fit for him but the silent and unhospitable wilderness.—PARKER.

THE CHURCH

"Christ loved the church, and gave himself for it, that he might sanctify and cleanse it, with the washing of the water by the word, that he might present it to himself a glorious church."—Eph. 5:23-27.

"Glorious things of thee are spoken,
  Zion, city of our God;
He, whose word cannot be broken.
  Formed thee for his own abode;
On the rock of ages founded,
  What can shake thy sure repose?
With salvation's wall surrounded,
  Thou may'st smile at all thy foes."
      —JOHN NEWTON.

PRESENT FOES TO FIGHT

The church ought to be the leader, the inspirer of the age. It is all folly for us to be discussing old issue—arraigning Nero, hanging Absalom, striking the Philistines with Shamgar's ox-goad—when all about us are iniquities to be slain—a corrupt legislature, a rotten judiciary, and a whiskey ring!—TALMAGE.

WHY CONDEMN THE CHURCH?

Do you ask, "Why not do away with the church, if its members make so many mistakes?" Would you take away the light-house because careless mariners, through wrong observations, run their ships high and dry upon the shore? Would you put out the lamps in your house because moths and millers burn their wings in it? What would the children do?—BEECHER.

DO NOT MAGNIFY TRIFLES

If a man should fire a house to destroy the mice in it, we should think him to be fairly mad. Yet those who consider themselves to be reasonable men will set the church in a blaze about the merest trifle. Meeting after meeting will be called, and angry discussions provoked, and holy work overturned about the smallest mistake of the preacher, on the minutest fault of the deacon. One would think that heaven itself were endangered, and yet it turns out to be a question of infinitessimal importance. Societies which were doing great service have often been broken up by the crazy whimsies of good brethren, who made much ado about nothing, and did great harm in trying to do a little good. Aim at reformation, not at desolation. The church has been thought to be sick, and fools have doctored it till they brought it to death's door by their poisons.—SPURGEON.

SOMETHING WRONG

Nine-tenths, at least, of the church members never think of speaking for Christ. If they see a man, perhaps a near relative, going right down to ruin, going rapidly, they never think of speaking to him about his sinful course, and of seeking to win him to Christ. Now certainly there must be something wrong, and yet when you talk with them, you find they have faith, and you can not say they are not children of God; but they have not the power, they have not the liberty, they have not the love that real disciples of Christ should have. A great many people are thinking that the church needs new measures, that it needs new buildings, that it needs new organs, that it needs new choirs, and all these new things. That is not what the church of God needs to-day. It is the old power that the Apostles had—that is what we want.—MOODY.

He has but one church; for the second Adam, like the first, is the husband of one wife. And just as the church cannot have two heads, neither can the head have two bodies; for, as that body were a monster which had more heads than one, not less monstrous were that form where one head was united to two separate bodies. Of all these churches, then, each claiming to be cast in the true gospel mould,—that with consecrated bishops, this with simple presbyters, this other without either; that administering baptism to infants as well as adults, this only to adults; that robed in a ritual of many forms, this thinking that religion, like beauty, when unadorned, is adorned the most—which is Christ's body, the Lamb's wife? which are we to receive as the favorite of heaven? Of which does God say as he said of David among rival brethren, "Arise, anoint her, for this is she?" Of none of them. Christ has a church, but it is none of these. In explanation of a remark which may surprise some, and is fitted to teach all of us humility and charity, I observe: that Christ's body which is not identical with any one church, is formed of all true believers, to whatever denomination they may belong.—GUTHRIE.

THE SOUL IMMORTAL

"And man became a living soul."—Gen. 2:7.

> The Witnesses are heard: the cause is o'er.
> Let conscience file the sentence in her court,
> Dearer than deeds that half a realm convey.
> Thus sealed by truth, the authentic record runs,
> Thus know, all—infidels! (unapt to know!)
> 'Tie immortality your nature solves;
> 'Tis immortality deciphers man.
> And opens all the mysteries of his make.
> Without it, half his instincts are a riddle;
> Without it, all his virtues are a dream.
> His very crimes attest his dignity;
> His sateless thirst for pleasure, gold and fame,
> Declares him born for blessings infinite.
> —EDWARD YOUNG.

THE IMMORTALITY OF INFLUENCE

It is the privilege of every man to live more in the future than he does in the present. John Wesley's name is a thousand fold greater to-day than it was when he was living. He still lives. He lives in the lives of thousands and millions of his followers.

Martin Luther lives more to-day than he did centuries ago, when he was living in Germany. He only lived one life for a while. But, now, look at the myriads of lives he is living. He is dead in the sight of the world, but "his works do follow him." He still lives.

The voice of John the Baptist is ringing through the world to-day, although nearly nineteen hundred years have passed away. Herod thought when he was beheading Him he was hushing His voice, but it is ringing all through the earth today. John the Baptist lives, because he lived for God. If a man just gets outside of himself and begins to work for God, his name will be immortal. Why, you may go to Scotland to-day, and you will find the influence of John Knox over every mountain. It seems that you can almost feel the breath of that man's prayer in Scotland today. His influence still lives.—MOODY.

STARS SYMBOLS OF IMMORTALITY

The same stars that look down on us looked down upon the Chaldean shepherds. The meteor that I saw flashing across the sky the other night, I wonder if it was not the same one that pointed down to where Jesus lay in a manger, and if, having pointed out his birth-place, it has ever since been wandering through the heavens, watching to see how the world would treat him. When Adam awoke in the garden, in the cool of the day, he saw coming out through the dusk of the evening the same worlds that greeted us on our way to church to-night.

In Independence Hall is an old cracked bell that sounded the signature of the Declaration of Independence. You can not ring it now; but this great chime of silvery bells that strike in the dome of night ring out with as sweet a tone as when God swung them at creation. Look up to-night, and know that the white lilies that bloom in the hanging gardens of our King are century plants—not blooming one© in a hundred years, but through all the centuries.

The star at which the mariner looks to-night was the light by which the ships of Tarshish was guided across the Mediterranean, and the Venetian flotilla found its way into Lepanto. Their armor is as bright to-night as when in ancient battle, the stars in their courses fought against Sisera. To the ancients, stars were the symbols of eternity. But here the figure breaks down—not in defeat, but on the majesties of the judgment. The stars shall not shine forever. The Bible says they shall fall like autumn leaves. It is almost impossible for a man to take in a courser going a mile in three minutes; but God shall take in the worlds, flying a hundred thousand miles an hour by one pull of his finger. As, when the factory band slips at nightfall from the main wheel, all the smaller wheels slacken their speed and with slower and slower motion they turn until they come to a full stop; so this great machinery of the universe, wheel within wheel, making revolutions of appalling speed, shall, by the touch of God's hand, slip the band of present law, and slacken, and stop. That is what will be the matter with the mountains. The chariots in which they ride shall halt so suddenly that the kings shall be thrown out. Star after star shall be carried out to burial amid the funeral torches of burning worlds. Constellations shall throw ashes on their head, and all up and down the highways of space shall be mourning, mourning, mourning, because the worlds are dead. But Christian workers shall never quit their thrones—they shall reign forever and ever. Forever the river of joy flows on; forever the jubilee progresses—forever, forever.—TALMAGE.

THE GRAIN OF WHEAT

On unrolling some of the old Egyptian mummies, you will find wheat three thousand years old. The Greek empire has risen and gone; the Roman empire has been riven and its dust has been blown away, and civilization has developed since the careful attendants rolled up that wheat; it has lain three thousand years doing nothing but keeping unconscious company with hideous mummies; and yet when taken out and planted in a field it goes to work, comes up, develops a stem, and brings forth fruit as though it had not taken a wink of sleep. And if wheat will keep as long as that, I am sure that men will. Though they are for years wrapped up, yet when God unrolls them the seed will come up and the germ grow again. Then let us take a broader view. Do not think of life as in the compass of a pint or a gill. Measure existence on a broader scale. How infinite the space! How enormous the duration! How transcendent the capacity which belongs to the human soul!—BEECHER.

IMMORTALITY COMMON TO CHRISTIAN AND HEATHEN MINDS

Why do these weeping Greeks approach the dead man, as he lies on his bier for burial, and open his mouth to put in an obolus? That coin is passage money for the surly ferryman who rows the spirit over Styx's stream. And why, in that forest grave, around which plumed and painted warriors stand unmoved and unmovable as statues, do they bury with the body of the Indian chief his canoe and bow and arrow. He goes to follow the chase and hunt the deer in the spectre land, where the Great Spirit lives, and the spirits of his fathers have gone before him. How easy it is to teach in these customs and beliefs a sort of rude copy of the words Life and Immortality. I shall not die but live.—GUTHRIE.

THE CHRISTIAN OUT OF DEATH'S REACH

The time will come when men will laugh at death. We shall one day get such a view of the universe that we shall look down upon death, and say, "O death, where is thy sting?" How so? Jesus Christ abolished death. He brought life and immortality to light. If we believe in Him, death will to us be no longer a spectre, a ghost, an ugly guest to the house, sucking out our blood, and darkening our future. It will then become a swinging door,— and, as it swings, we shall pass in to light, to music, to rest. Death will always be a frightful thing to the man who has no Savior. He may have lived himself into that measure of beasthood that will not confess terror. I never knew of a felled ox saying, "Death is very terrible." So there are men who have lived themselves down so beastward and devilward that they hardly know death from life. But the man who is in Christ, his life is above the reach of death. When the body crumbles and falls down, to get up no more, the soul is a guest in Heaven. A guest? Nay, —he is a child at Home!—PARKER.

TONGUE

"Refrain thy tongue from evil."—1 Pet. 3:10.

"Five things observe with care:
Of whom you speak,
To whom you speak,
And how, and when, and where."

"WHISPERS"

When Paul called the list of the world's villainy, he put in the midst of the roll "Whisperers." They are so-called because they generally speak undervoice, and in a confidential way, their hand to the side of the mouth, acting as a funnel to keep the precious information from wandering into the wrong ear. They speak softly, not because they have lack of lung force, of because they are overpowered with the spirit of gentleness, but because they want to escape the consequences of defamation. If no one hears but the person whispered unto, and the speaker be arraigned, he can deny the whole thing, for whisperers are always first-class liars! Some people whisper because they are hoarse from a cold, or because they wish to convey some useful information without disturbing others, but the slanderer gives muffled utterance from sinister and depraved motive, and sometimes you can only hear the sibilant sound as the letter "S" drops from the tongue into the listening ear, the brief hiss of the serpent as it projects its venom.

From the frequency with which Paul speaks of them under different titles, I conclude that he must have suffered somewhat from them. His personal appearance was defective, and that made him perhaps the target of this ridicule. And besides that, he was a bachelor, persisting in his celibacy down into the sixties, indeed, all the way through; and some having failed in their connubial designs upon him, the little missionary was put under the raking fires of these whisperers. He was no doubt a rare morsel for their scandalization; and he cannot keep his patience any longer, and he lays hold of these miscreants of the tongue, and gives them a very hard setting down in the text among the scoundrels and murderers.

They are to be found everywhere, these whisperers. I think their paradise is a country village of about one or two thousand people, where everybody knows everybody else. But they are also to be found in our cities. They have a prying disposition. They look into the basement windows at the tables of their neighbors, and can tell just what they have to eat, morning and night. They can see as far through a key-hole as other people can see with the door wide open. They can hear conversation on the opposite side of the room. The world to them is a whispering gallery. —TALMAGE.

UNKIND WORDS LIKE NEEDLES

I saw in the museum at Venice an instrument with which one of the old Italian tyrants was wont to shoot poisoned needles at the objects of his wanton malignity. I thought of gossips, backbiters, and secret slanderers, and wished that their mischievous devices might come to a speedy end. Their weapons of innuendo, shrug, and whispers, appear to be insignificant as needles, but the venom which they instill is deadly to many a reputation.—SPURGEON.

One of our ancient nobility had inscribed over his castle gate these words, which I commend to all persons who are thin-skinned in the matter of private gossip or public worship:

THEY SAY.
WHAT DO THEY SAY?
LET THEM SAY.

—IBID.

A DEADLY SIN

Jesus calls a slanderous spirit a beam, compared with which any other mistake is a little thin splinter. Here is a man that condemns every poor creature that is overtaken in a fault. He has no sympathy with such. The man took a glass of whisky too much, lost his equilibrium, was seen in a reeling state—that circumstance is reported to the man who only indulges in slanderous criticism, and the man immediately calls for the excommunication of the erring brother from the church, not knowing that he himself is drunk, but not with wine, drunk with a hostile spirit, drunk with uncharitableness.

If I had been guilty of this ineffable meanness, I would preach to myself as loudly and keenly as to any other man,—if I had been guilty of speaking an unkind word about any human creature, or suspecting the honesty of any man. If ever I had said about a brother minister, "He is a fine man in many respects, a noble creature, kind, chivalrous, grand of soul, but—," if ever I have said that but, God will punish me for it.

We do not lay hold of this great truth sufficiently. We think that a little slander is of no consequence. To be called up before the church and condemned for slander! Condemn the drunkard, turn out the man who by infinite pressure has committed some sin—turn him out—certainly, and never go after him, and never care what becomes of him, let a wolf gnaw him—only get rid of him:—if we go home and speak unkindly of man, woman, or child, who is the great sinner; the drunkard we have just expelled, or the closely-shaven, highly-polished Christian who does nothing but filch his neighbor's good name?—PARKER.

WOMAN

"And they marveled that He was speaking with the woman." —John 4:27.

"O, what is woman, what her smile,
    Her lip of love, her eye of light?
What is she if her lip revile
    The lowly Jesus? Love may write
His name upon her marble brow,
    Or linger in her curls of jet;
The bright spring flowers may scarcely bow
    Beneath her step, and yet—and yet,
Without that meeker grace, she'll be
    A lighter thing than vanity."

WOMEN AMONG HEATHEN

Now what is the difference between the condition of women there and here, then and now? The only difference is that which is made by the gospel of the Son of God. O, women! To-day you would have been hitched to the. plough, or you would have been leaping upon the funeral-pyre, or you would have been ground under the heel of man's cruelty and insolence, were it not for the fact that in this land and in this age the Lord Jesus Christ appeared, with love in his voice and omnipotence in his arm, and stood above this grave of womanhood, and said, "forth!" And she has come forth in the dignity of a Christian hope.—TALMAGE.

WOMEN ON THE BATTLEFIELD

There never was a better illustration given of how well women can help in the camp, if she tries to, than during our late war. Men forged the cannon. Men fashioned the musketry. Men manned the guns. Men unlimbered the batteries. Men lifted the wounded into the ambulances. But women scraped the lint. Women administered the cordials. Women watched the dying pillow. Women wrote the last messages of love to the home circle. A woman was the mourner; the only mourner at many a burial.— IBID.

A LOST WOMAN

Look out upon that fallen creature whose gay sally through the street calls out the significant laugh of bad men, the pity of good men, and the horror of the pure. Was not her cradle as pure as ever a loved infant found? Love soothed its cries. Sisters watched its peaceful sleepy and a mother pressed it fondly to her bosom. Had you afterwards when spring flowers covered the earth, and every gale was odor, and every sound was music, seen her fairer than the lily or the violet, searching them, would you not have said, "Sooner shall the rose grow poisonous than she; both may wither, but neither corrupt." And how often, at evening, did she clasp her tiny hands in prayer! How often did she put the wonder-raising questions to her mother, of God, and heaven, and the dead, as if she had seen heavenly things in a vision! As young womanhood advanced, and these foreshadowed graces ripened to the bud and burst into bloom, health glowed in her cheek, love looked from her eye, and purity was an atmosphere around her. Alas, she forsook the guide of her youth! Faint thoughts of evil, like a far-off cloud which the sunset gilds, came first; nor does the rosy sunset blush deeper along the heaven, than her cheek at the first thought of evil. Now, ah, mother, and thou guiding elder sister, could you have seen the lurking spirit embosomed in that cloud, a holy prayer might have broken the spell, a tear have washed its stain! Alas, they saw it not! She spoke it not; she was forsaking the guide of her youth. She thinketh no more of heaven. She breatheth no more prayers. She hath no more penitential tears to shed, she drops the bitter tear upon the cheek of despair,—then her only suitor. Thou hast forsaken the covenant of thy God. Go down! fall never to rise! Hell opens to be thy home! —BEECHER.

HEROISM OF CHRISTIAN WOMEN

Both before and since the days when they ministered to our Lord, followed him to Calvary with their tears, were last at the cross and first at the sepulchre, the church has exhibited many instances of high and holy heroism on the part of women. However deserving of the name in ordinary circumstances where martyr's fires were fiercely burning, and scaffolds flowed with blood, and prisons overflowed with captives, women have not showed themselves to be the "weaker sex." On the contrary, when adherence to principle involved painful sacrifices, men have found such support in gentle women, as I have seen the green and pliant ivy lend the wall it clung to, when that, undermined and shaken, was ready to fall.—GUTHRIE.

CHRIST AND WOMAN

You cannot get rid of Christ. You exclude Him from your schools by act of Parliament, but, passing through the midst of you, He says, "Suffer Me and the children to meet; let the flowers see the sun;" you find Him in statute-books, in philanthropic institutions, in literature; you find Him now just as his disciples found Him, in out-of-the-way places, doing out-of-the-way things;—"they marvelled that he spake with the WOMAN,"—the eternal marvel, the eternal hope! He is speaking with the woman still; speaking with her in India, in China, in islands far out upon the sea; presently He will take up her children in his arms and bless them, and be himself as the child that is born unto every woman.—PARKER.

YOUTH

"Remember now thy Creator in the days of thy youth."—Eccles. 12:1.

There are gains for all our losses,
    There are balms for all our pain,
But when youth, the dream departs,
It takes something from our hearts,
    And it never comes again.
        —-RICHARD H. STODDARD.

Ah, five and twenty years ago
    Had I but planted seed of trees,
How now I should enjoy their shade,
    And see their fruit swing in the breeze.
        —ORIENTAL.

In an election, the first votes recorded count all the day long, and so encourage the party through all the anxious hours of polling. When men give in their names for Jesus and his cause in the morning of their lives, their whole existence influences their time, and their encouragement to the cause is life-long. Young people, remember this!— SPURGEON.

A soul that comes early to Christ is worth more to itself and to the world than a soul that comes late to Christ, and not so much perhaps because it wants to serve God, as because it is afraid it will go to hell.

NEGLIGENCE OF THE CHURCH

The world comes to the child when it is in the April of life, and sows tares. The world comes along again when the child is in the May of life, and sows thistles. Again in the fair June it comes and sows nox vomica. The church meanwhile folds its hands and waits until the April has gone, and the May has gone, and June and July have gone, and then at the close of August gets in earnest and says, "Now, now we have got a bag of good wheat here, and we must sow it in this fresh young soil, and we shall have a glorious harvest!" Will it? No, no! It is too late! Everlastingly too late! You should have sowed in April and in May the good seed of the kingdom.

PATIENCE WITH YOUTH

As we get older, do not let us be affronted if young men and women crowd us a little. We will have had our day, and we must let them have theirs. When our voices get cracked, let us not snarl at those who can warble. When our knees are stiffened, let us have patience with those who go fleet as the deer. Because our leaf is fading, do not let us despise the unfrosted.—TALMAGE.

INSIDIOUS TEMPTATIONS

The young are seldom tempted to outright wickedness; evil comes to them as an enticement. The honest generosity and fresh heart of youth would refuse to embrace open meanness and undisguised vice. The adversary conforms his wiles to their nature. He tempts them to the basest deeds by beginning with innocent ones, gliding to more exceptionable, and, finally, to positively wicked ones. All our warnings therefore must be against the vernal beauty of vice! Its autumn and winter none wish.

THE DECEITFUL NATURE OF SIN

The face of pleasure to the youthful imagination is the face of an angel, a paradise of smiles, a home of love; while the rugged face of industry, imbrowned by toil, is dull and repulsive; but at the end it is not so. These are harlot charms which pleasure wears. At last, when industry shall put on her beautiful garments, and rest in the palace which her own hands have built, pleasure, blotched and diseased with indulgence, shall lie down and die upon the dung-hill.—BEECHER.

ADVICE TO YOUNG CHRISTIANS

Now we want these young converts to serve Christ. It is not too much to expect that each of you should bring twelve more. One young man came to me and said he was converted on the 3d of February; he had a list of fifty-nine persons, with the residence of each, whom he had since that time been instrumental in leading to Christ; and if that young convert had led fifty-nine, every man, woman, and child ought to be able to reach some. Let each one go to work. That is the way to grow in strength. "They that water others shall themselves be watered, and the liberal soul shall be fed. God is able to make all grace abound." Let me give you a little advice. Let your friends be those who are in the church. Select for your companions experienced Christians. Keep company with those who know a little more than you do yourselves. Of course, you get the best of the bargain; but from my own experience I know it is the best way to make advances in religious life. And get in love with the Book, and the world will lose its hold on you.—MOODY.

An address to converts at the close of a great revival In New York.

INFLUENCE OF A MOTHER ON YOUTH

Take the history of Rehaboam. There is, in his life, just one short sentence which supplies the key, more perhaps than anything else, to his sin and folly,—"his mother's name was Naamah, an Ammonitess." She was by blood an alien, and by religion a heathen. Unhappy in many things, but unhappiest most in such a mother, he begins to be regarded more with pity than with astonishment. The letters written on water are hardly formed when they are filled up; on the other hand the finger that traces them on stone leaves no visible impression on its indurated service; but plastic clay, midway between what is hard and soft, offers to the gentlest finger a substance which both receives and retains an impression. Such is the heart that youth and childhood offer to a mother's influence. Hear how Cowper sings of the boy by a mother's knee.—

> "His heart, now passive, yields to thy command,
> Secure it thine, its key is in thine hand."

—GUTHRIE.

www.ingramcontent.com/pod-product-compliance
Lightning Source LLC
Chambersburg PA
CBHW061633040426
42446CB00010B/1400